To all the young people (and young at heart)
who want to change the world for the better
Yx

To Mum, for making me feel like I could do anything
that I set my mind to
A

Specialist edits by Sofia Akel,
Race Equity Researcher and Black Studies Lecturer

Text copyright © 2023 by Yassmin Abdel-Magied
Illustrations copyright © 2023 by Aleesha Nandhra

First US edition 2024

Library of Congress Catalog Card Number 2022923369
ISBN 978-1-5362-3133-5

23 24 25 26 27 28 CCP 10 9 8 7 6 5 4 3 2 1

Printed in Shenzhen, Guangdong, China

This book was typeset in News Gothic Std.
The illustrations were done in mixed media.

Walker Books US
a division of
Candlewick Press
99 Dover Street
Somerville, Massachusetts 02144

www.walkerbooksus.com

MIX
Paper | Supporting
responsible forestry
FSC® C008047
FSC
www.fsc.org

YASSMIN ABDEL-MAGIED

STAND UP AND
SPEAK OUT
AGAINST
RACISM

ILLUSTRATED BY ALEESHA NANDHRA

WALKER BOOKS

CONTENTS

INTRODUCTION   8

ABOUT THIS BOOK   10

HOW DID RACISM START?   13

CHAPTER 1
WHY DOES RACISM EXIST?   14

CHAPTER 2
IS RACISM DIFFERENT IN EVERY COUNTRY?   24

CHAPTER 3
WHY DOES RACISM STILL EXIST?   28

CHAPTER 4
WHAT IS THE DIFFERENCE BETWEEN MY "RACE." "NATIONALITY."
AND "ETHNICITY"?   34

CHAPTER 5
IS PREJUDICE THE SAME AS RACISM?   38

CHAPTER 6
WHAT ABOUT DISCRIMINATION TOWARD RELIGIOUS GROUPS?   42

RACISM TODAY 47

CHAPTER 7
HOW DOES RACISM WORK? 50

CHAPTER 8
WHAT DOES RACISM LOOK LIKE TODAY? 64

CHAPTER 9
WHY DOES REPRESENTATION MATTER? 70

CHAPTER 10
WHAT IS STEREOTYPING, AND WHY IS IT BAD? 72

CHAPTER 11
WHAT IS JUSTICE? 76

HOW TO STAND UP AND SPEAK OUT 79

CHAPTER 12
WHY SHOULD I CARE ABOUT RACISM WHEN THERE ARE SO MANY
OTHER THINGS GOING ON? 82

CHAPTER 13
HOW DO YOU UNDO STEREOTYPES? 86

CHAPTER 14
ALL THE REALLY BAD STUFF HAPPENED SO LONG AGO.
I DIDN'T DO IT. WHY SHOULD I CARE? IT'S NOT MY FAULT! 88

CHAPTER 15
WHERE DO I START? 89

CHAPTER 16
HOW CAN I ADDRESS INTERNALIZED RACISM? 90

CHAPTER 17
INTERPERSONAL: WHAT SHOULD I DO IF I SEE ACTS OF RACISM HAPPEN IN FRONT OF ME? 92

CHAPTER 18
HOW CAN I ENCOURAGE OTHERS TO BE ANTI-RACIST, INCLUDING MY PARENTS OR TEACHER? 96

CHAPTER 19
WHAT SHOULD I DO IF SOMEONE IS RACIST TO ME? 98

CHAPTER 20
MY FRIEND SAID I WAS RACIST TO THEM, BUT I DIDN'T MEAN TO BE! HOW CAN I BE RACIST IF I DIDN'T MEAN IT? 100

CHAPTER 21
WHY DOES IT GET WEIRD WHEN YOU POINT OUT SOMETHING IS RACIST? 104

CHAPTER 22
I'M WHITE BUT MY LIFE HASN'T BEEN EASY! HOW COME PEOPLE CAN SAY THINGS TO ME AND IT'S NOT CONSIDERED RACIST? 108

CHAPTER 23
CAN YOU BE RACIST IF YOU ARE NOT WHITE?   110

CHAPTER 24
I DON'T HAVE ANYBODY WHO IS DIFFERENT FROM ME IN
MY SCHOOL OR TOWN. WHAT CAN I DO TO FIGHT RACISM?   112

CHAPTER 25
WHAT ABOUT INSTITUTIONAL RACISM?   114

CHAPTER 26
WHY IS RACISM SO HARD TO STOP?   116

HOW TO GET INSPIRED   120

GLOSSARY   122

INDEX   126

INTRODUCTION

HELLO THERE! I'M YASSMIN ABDEL-MAGIED, AND I'M SO EXCITED YOU'RE READING THIS BOOK.

I was born in Sudan, brought up in Meeanjin (present-day Brisbane, Australia), and now live in London, the capital city of the United Kingdom. In the UK, I am considered a Black (African) woman. I also wear the hijab as part of my practice as a Muslim woman. There's a lot going on! But I'm more than just my "race" (Black), ethnicity (Sudanese), language group (Arabic), visa status (immigrant), or gender (cis woman). I'm also an engineer (I've designed my own race car), a writer (this is my fifth book), and an advocate for social justice. For me, social justice is about making the world fairer and safer for us all. That's why I decided to write this book. Right now, we live in a world where life is like climbing up a big, tall, scary mountain, and when we are born, we all get a different set of tools to climb it.

OTHERS HAVE TO USE THE STAIRS.

SOME PEOPLE GET ACCESS TO A CABLE CAR.

SOME PEOPLE HAVE THEIR WAY BLOCKED.

IMAGINARY MOUNTAIN OF LIFE

THE LUCKIEST GET A JETPACK.

It doesn't seem very fair, does it?

This book focuses on how "race" and racism affect the way different people go up the mountain, depending on the group (in this case "race") they have been put into.

How can we make the climb fair for everyone?

I visited young people in schools around the UK and asked what they wanted to know about racism and how to fight for racial justice.

Each chapter in this book answers some of their questions, and many more. What you learn will help you understand why racism exists, how it plays out, and what we can all do about it so that Earth is a safer, fairer place for us all, inshallah!

SOME PEOPLE HAVE TO WEAR BACKPACKS WEIGHED DOWN WITH LEAD.

> "Inshallah" is an Arabic word meaning "God willing." It's used by Muslims and Arabic speakers of many religions to talk about events we hope will happen in the future. It's like a version of "Fingers crossed!"

ABOUT THIS BOOK

STAND UP AND SPEAK OUT AGAINST RACISM IS SPLIT INTO THREE MAIN SECTIONS.

The first deals with **how racism started**: where it came from and why it exists. It talks about the history, over hundreds of years, to help explain the background to racism.

Section two is all about **what racism looks like today**. You will learn about the four different ways racism shows up, as well as the impact of racism on the daily lives of everyday people, like you and me!

The final section is all about action: **How do we stand up and speak out against racism?** Here you will find tactics, tips, and tricks to help you get started, as well as answers to many of the questions young people asked me about this challenging topic. And speaking of challenging topics, I want to give you a heads-up before we begin.

Racism can be a heavy issue to discuss, whoever you are. Some of what you read in this book might make you feel sad or uncomfortable, or bring up feelings of guilt, shame, anger, and frustration. That is OK. It is normal to feel heavy emotions when it comes to topics like this. My advice?

First: Remember to breathe. If you are feeling really intense emotions, it is fine to put the book down and take at least three long, deep breaths. I always find this calming when I get a bit stressed out.

Second: Notice what it is you are feeling and ask yourself where that feeling has come from. Are you remembering a moment when you were on the receiving end of a racist act? Are you feeling guilty about something you said?

Third: Find a way to express that emotion safely. Maybe write down how you are feeling, or speak to a trusted adult or knowledgeable friend. It can be helpful to read this book alongside another person so you have someone else to turn to and discuss what you are learning.

> You'll see boxes like this throughout the book, giving you extra pieces of interesting information and asking questions to get you thinking more deeply about the things you've discovered.

OTHER NOTES

- You don't have to read this book cover to cover, from front to back. Take it little by little, put it down if it gets to be too much, think about what you are learning, and come back to it when it feels right. We are all on a journey, and we can all take it at our own pace.

- If you see a word underlined in **_bold italics_**, you can turn to the glossary (pages 122–125) to learn its definition. There are also pages at the back (120–121) where you'll find further information about inspiring people or groups who have resisted the impacts of racial injustice.

OK! YOU READY? LET'S GET INTO IT!

HOW DID RACISM START?

CHAPTER 1

WHY DOES RACISM EXIST?

Hundreds of years ago, there wasn't such a thing as "race" or "racism." Then some cunning people came up with a way to group people together to gain power, control, and money.

> WHAT ARE YOU TALKING ABOUT, YASSMIN?! HOW DOES WHETHER PEOPLE THINK I'M BLACK OR WHITE OR SOMETHING ELSE HAVE ANYTHING TO DO WITH MONEY?

Why, I'm glad you asked. From the fifteenth century onward, European countries like Spain, Portugal, France, Belgium, Germany, the Netherlands, and England sailed around the world and started **<u>colonizing</u>** other countries. They captured people, stealing them away from their homes, **<u>enslaving</u>** them, forcing them to work for free under terrible conditions. They also traded people as if they were property: the more people you "owned" (or enslaved), the wealthier you were. It was pretty grim. The Europeans needed some way of justifying all the bad things they were doing to make it sound . . . legit, and not as awful as it actually was. Some of what they did included . . .

putting people into different groups called "races" based on physical features like skin color, hair texture—or even the size of their heads . . .

saying that people of some "races" were better than others (which obviously wasn't true) . . .

introducing laws targeting people based on the groups the Europeans had created, like saying that "Black" people could be considered property and so didn't have rights like "white" people.

The idea of different "races" started because European countries wanted ways to control and make money off of people from other places around the world without feeling like they were doing a bad thing. If some people were less human than you, then it was all OK, right?

Of course, it was not OK. Sadly, it took a long time for Europeans to change their ways because this way of doing things had been presented as "normal" and "civilized" by those in power. By the time laws started to change, the damage was done.

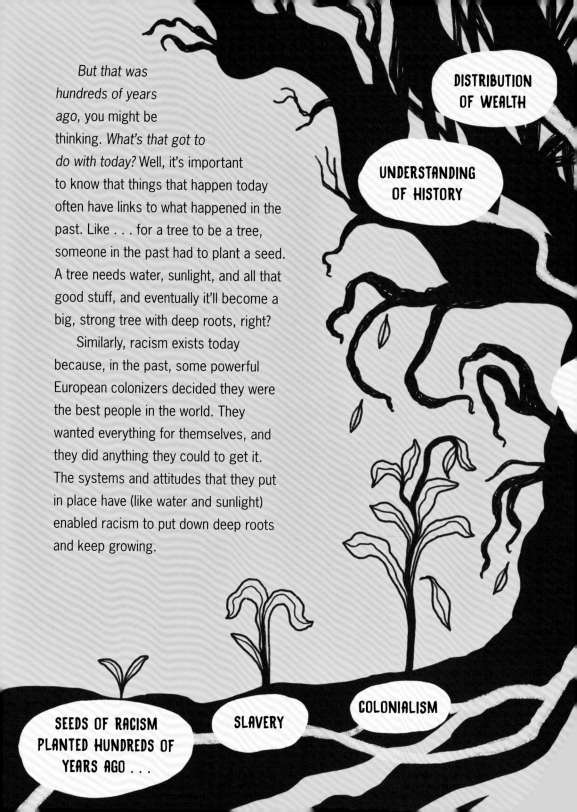

But that was hundreds of years ago, you might be thinking. *What's that got to do with today?* Well, it's important to know that things that happen today often have links to what happened in the past. Like . . . for a tree to be a tree, someone in the past had to plant a seed. A tree needs water, sunlight, and all that good stuff, and eventually it'll become a big, strong tree with deep roots, right?

Similarly, racism exists today because, in the past, some powerful European colonizers decided they were the best people in the world. They wanted everything for themselves, and they did anything they could to get it. The systems and attitudes that they put in place have (like water and sunlight) enabled racism to put down deep roots and keep growing.

DISTRIBUTION OF WEALTH

UNDERSTANDING OF HISTORY

SEEDS OF RACISM PLANTED HUNDREDS OF YEARS AGO . . .

SLAVERY

COLONIALISM

ATTITUDES PASSED DOWN THROUGH EACH GENERATION

MANY, MANY MORE ISSUES—SOME BIG, SOME SMALL, BUT ALL OF THEM IMPORTANT

RACISM TODAY

IS IT TRUE?

Were Europeans the only people hungry for power, control, and money? Of course not! Throughout history, there have been people from many different *imperialist* societies who invaded lands, stole wealth, and *oppressed* others for their own gain. There was Genghis Khan of the Mongol Empire, the Tang dynasty of China, the tsars of the Russian Empire, and many, many more. Power-hungry people exist in every society. The important thing to remember about the conversation about racism, and why we focus on the Europeans, is that we are still living with the *legacy* of European colonialism today.

SLAVERY AND COLONIZATION WENT ON FOR HUNDREDS OF YEARS, SO IT WILL TAKE US A WHILE (AND A LOT OF WORK) TO UNDO IT ALL. BUT THAT'S WHY WE NEED YOUR HELP TO MAKE THINGS BETTER!

DID YOU KNOW?

The English were among the first to codify, or put into law, the idea of a "white race" and a "Black race." In 1661, English colonizers created something known as the Barbados Slave Code. It stated that if you were "Black," you were "owned" and didn't have any rights as a human being. The law gave white people the right to torture and murder Black people without facing any punishment. Rules like these slave codes formed the roots of the racist world we live in today.

The codes also served a second purpose. They divided Black people from other workers. Even if they did the same job, non-Black workers had a higher status than Black workers. This is a classic divide-and-conquer strategy! So rather than everyone teaming up to fight the slave owners, they would turn against and resent each other. That is another thing that racism does that we need to fight: it makes us turn on each other rather than focus on working together to pull out the roots of _discrimination_. This still happens today. It's super sneaky . . . and super wrong.

Divide and Conquer

Imagine you and your nine best friends work at a shoe factory making fancy, expensive shoes. Instead of paying you, the owner of the factory gives you all five pairs of shoes that you have to share among yourselves. You fight and fight over who worked harder, over who looks best in them, over who deserves the shoes. Yet you and your friends never question the owner of the factory, who has hundreds—thousands—of shoes, about why they are keeping them all for themselves. By making you fight against one another, you get distracted from the real injustice: that you are not being paid properly for your work. This is called "divide and conquer," and it's a terrible, horrible tactic. Watch out for its poison!

HAVE YOU HEARD OF THE "SCRAMBLE FOR AFRICA"?

IS THAT A BOARD GAME?

I'M AFRAID IT'S SOMETHING A LOT MORE SERIOUS THAN THAT . . .

In the late 1880s, European countries were becoming more and more interested in taking what they could get from the continent of Africa. They had stolen people (through slavery), but that wasn't enough. They wanted the natural resources too—the sugar and the rubber and the gold. Rather than fight each other for resources, they came up with a pretty gross plan.

In November 1884, the first chancellor of Germany invited thirteen European powers, along with the United States, to Berlin to discuss how to split Africa up among them. Note, not a single African person was invited, and the interests of the African people were pretty much ignored in this whole process.

Beforehand, Europeans had only settled on the coast, but by the end of the Berlin Conference, they had "claimed" almost the entire continent. Before the Europeans arrived, the people who lived in Africa had their own ways of organizing themselves, depending on their **_ethnic group_**, language, or ancestors.

The Europeans just came in, drew some lines on a map, and said, "This is now a country!" They didn't care that the people who actually lived there didn't want to be controlled by some random Europeans. They just cared about getting more resources for their empires. They drew lines straight through tribal areas, split up communities, and generally made a total mess.

By the start of the First World War, almost all of Africa had been seized and divided up along borders that Africans played no part in deciding. This map gives you an idea of which countries, or empires, claimed to "own" which regions of Africa. It also shows the few areas of Africa that remained **_autonomous_**: Aussa, Ethiopia, Kongo, Liberia, and Mbunda.

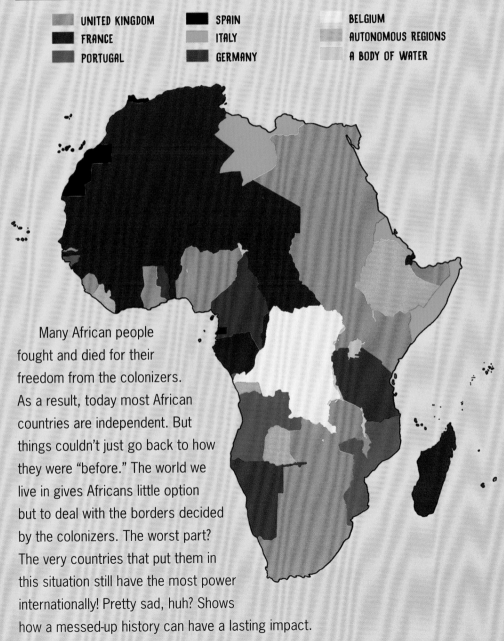

UNITED KINGDOM	SPAIN	BELGIUM
FRANCE	ITALY	AUTONOMOUS REGIONS
PORTUGAL	GERMANY	A BODY OF WATER

Many African people fought and died for their freedom from the colonizers. As a result, today most African countries are independent. But things couldn't just go back to how they were "before." The world we live in gives Africans little option but to deal with the borders decided by the colonizers. The worst part? The very countries that put them in this situation still have the most power internationally! Pretty sad, huh? Shows how a messed-up history can have a lasting impact.

DID YOU KNOW?

There is NO accepted number of "races." This is because "race" is a social invention (made up by people) rather than a biological reality, so there's no test you can do to find out what "race" you are. And there are no agreed categories. People don't agree on what makes a person Black, or brown, or white, or Asian, or even if those are the correct categories to use! What's important to remember is that today's idea of "race" was created— and sustained—to justify treating people as lesser and using them to benefit European and imperialist countries. Without colonizing and enslaving people to do all the work, these countries wouldn't have been able to get so rich and powerful. It's easy to make a profit if you don't pay anyone!

TREAT ALL
PEOPLE
EQUALLY

There are often more differences within a so-called racial group than between groups. For example, if you have European ancestry, you might have more in common genetically with an Asian person than another European.

And did you know that many of the scientific studies that look into genetics have found that all people share over 99 percent of our DNA with each other? Even though we may look different, we are much, *much* more similar than we are different. Many differences come from the environment and other external factors and not our core biology. Cool, huh?

We don't need people to be the same as us to care that we are all treated with the same respect and care.

REMEMBER—EVEN IF "RACE" ISN'T REAL, RACIALIZATION AND RACISM DO EXIST. BUT BECAUSE THE IDEA WAS CREATED BY HUMANS, HUMAN BEINGS CAN GET RID OF IT TOO.

CHAPTER 2

IS RACISM DIFFERENT IN EVERY COUNTRY?

The Europeans used the belief that one "race" is better than all the rest to colonize countries all around the world without having to feel too guilty about it. That means racism was spread to a lot of different countries. Given how widely Europeans traveled, they spread their racism to most countries in the world. It's definitely not the exact same in every place, BUT wherever you are in the world, the simplest way to think about racism is that it is racial **_prejudice_** backed by power. The thing is, who is in power can look different depending on the history of the country and who is (and was) the **_dominant culture_**.

DOMINANT CULTURE

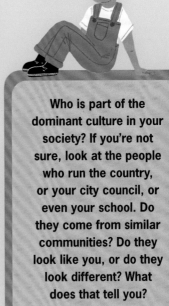

The dominant culture (usually—but not always—the majority) has the most power in society. The people in this group are in charge of institutions like the government, police, military, media, and education. They often decide what behaviors, values, and traditions are considered "normal" and "acceptable" in that society.

On the other hand, a historically **marginalized community** is a group of people who are outside the dominant culture or group. Often, if you are outside the dominant culture—even if there are a lot of you—you have less power, opportunity, and safety in society. For some groups, things have improved slightly over the years, but we still have a ways to go until we get a truly fair world.

Who is part of the dominant culture in your society? If you're not sure, look at the people who run the country, or your city council, or even your school. Do they come from similar communities? Do they look like you, or do they look different? What does that tell you?

COLORISM

Sometimes, especially in countries without majority-white populations, the issue is **colorism**, which is the discrimination against people with darker skin. Pre-colonization, this could often reflect wealth and class differences: if you had darker skin, it might indicate that you worked outside in the sun, and if you had lighter skin, that you likely had enough money to stay inside or came from a higher-class family. This attitude, mixed with the **white supremacist hierarchy** of the Europeans, meant being white was viewed as "better" and has left us in a world where people with lighter skin are viewed more favorably than others. But we know this is wrong! All shades of skin are wonderful and beautiful.

AS YOU CAN IMAGINE, OUR DIFFERENT HISTORIES MEAN THAT RACISM CAN BE EXPERIENCED DIFFERENTLY ALL OVER THE WORLD . . . SO IT'S IMPORTANT TO LISTEN TO PEOPLE'S EXPERIENCES RATHER THAN ASSUME YOU KNOW WHAT IT'S LIKE FOR THEM.

AUSTRALIA

Racism in the land now known as Australia is very much related to how the colonizers treated the **_Indigenous_**— or **_First Nations_**—people there. The British violently invaded, killing tens of thousands of people, and did not even consider a **_treaty_** with the First Nations peoples. Many Indigenous people today are understandably still quite angry about it. Furthermore, Australia operated under the White Australia policy, set up to stop any non-"white" Europeans from **_migrating_** to Australia. It wasn't until the 1970s that these policies ended!

UNITED STATES OF AMERICA

In the United States, many Black people are descendants of people taken into **_chattel slavery_**. Their ancestors were taken from their homes and families and deliberately cut off from their history and culture. The US also violently colonized **_Native nations_** and did not honor treaties with them. And in the nineteenth century, many Americans frustrated with low pay and lack of jobs wrongly blamed Chinese workers. It is a common tactic, blaming migrants for issues in society, and it has long-lasting consequences. The 1882 Chinese Exclusion Act stopped Chinese people from migrating to the US and becoming **_citizens_**. This finally changed in 1943.

BRAZIL

Brazil is another country whose **_racialized_** population is deeply connected to a brutal history of slavery. Made a colony of Portugal in 1500, Brazil brought in an estimated four to six million enslaved people over 350 years. That's more enslaved Africans than any other country in the world. Today, the descendants of these enslaved people are still fighting for **_justice_** and the chance to tell their own stories.

Out of the 195 countries in the world, how many were colonized and how many were colonizers? Why not do a little research and find out? Make two different lists . . . What do you notice?

BRITAIN

Contrary to popular belief, Black people have lived in Britain for a very long time. According to historian David Olusoga, people of African descent have been present in Britain for more than 1,700 years. However, the racism that exists in the UK today is connected to the way the British Empire used the idea of "race" to get more money and power. British people traveled across the world, invading and stealing, but whenever people from those countries wanted to travel to the UK, they were often denied entry. The UK introduced the Aliens Act in 1905 to stop what the government said were "undesirable" people from entering the country. As the years went by, they made it more and more difficult for people from the colonies to come to the UK, and if any did (or were invited in, like those who came on the HMT *Empire Windrush* ship), they were often treated badly, not given jobs, and sometimes **_deported_**. These things still happen today.

CHAPTER 3

WHY DOES RACISM STILL EXIST?

Remember how we talked about planting a seed? Imagine you planted a seed, only to discover, years later, that it was for a poisonous plant rather than a nice mango tree like you'd thought. Sadly, you can't Ctrl+Z a seed. There's no way to take the seed out of the ground and throw it away, because after all these years, it's changed into something completely different—a tree! And the way to get rid of a tree is very different from how you might get rid of a seed. That's how it is with racism—if enough powerful people back in the fifteenth century had said, "Hey, everyone, STOP putting people into groups called 'races' and making laws that treat some of those 'races' really badly!" things might be different. But unfortunately, that didn't happen. Even worse, the world got used to it. People began to think the fields of poisonous plants had always existed, rather than remembering that, a long time ago, someone planted those seeds . . .

The work of getting rid of racism began many years ago, so fortunately we aren't starting from scratch. Some of the bigger branches have already been "cut off," like when people worked together to legally end, or _**abolish**_, slavery across many parts of the British Empire in the 1830s and across the United States in the 1860s. Other branches of racism, like racist laws in parts of the US, were brought down by the civil rights movement in the 1950s and 1960s.

An incredible amount of time, effort, and organizing went into cutting down these branches, but the work isn't done yet. In order to truly get rid of racism, we have to carry on cutting down all the branches, chopping and grinding the trunks holding the branches up, AND pulling out all of the deep knotty roots; otherwise, the poisonous plants will simply grow back.

Why do you think people might want racism to continue? Why do you think it's hard to get rid of racism today? Who do you think is doing a good job? Who do you think might need to do more?

CUTTING DOWN ALL THE BRANCHES OF RACISM

UPROOTING RACISM— WORKING TOWARD RACIAL JUSTICE

The groups in power gave themselves a serious and pretty unfair head start up that Imaginary Mountain of Life. It was as if they whizzed straight to the top using rocket-propelled jetpacks, fueled by the blood, sweat, and tears of the people whose countries they colonized—and put lead into the backpacks of everyone else. That kind of head start doesn't just disappear—it's repeated with every generation. We have a lot of work to do to close the gap, and we have to do it together.

BUT WHAT KINDS OF THINGS GAVE THESE GROUPS SUCH A HEAD START?

CREATING WHITE SUPREMACY

Well, all the things we've discussed in this chapter that feed the roots of racism also provide fuel for the jetpack.

STEALING AND CONTROLLING BLACK AND BROWN PEOPLE'S RESOURCES (EVEN IN THEIR OWN HOMES)

SEIZING
LAND

TRANSFERRING THE WEALTH FROM COLONIALISM OVER HUNDREDS OF YEARS

ENSLAVING PEOPLE AND PREVENTING THEM FROM EARNING MONEY OR OWNING LAND

DESTROYING OTHER PEOPLE'S CULTURES

Slave Compensation Act

Many stately homes around the UK, including nearly one-third of current National Trust historic properties, benefited from colonialism and slavery. Lots of these huge houses contain items that were either taken from former colonies or bought with money connected to the enslavement of people. Numerous banks in the UK have links to—and made money from—slavery as well. But if you think that's bad, it gets worse. In 1837, the UK passed the Slave Compensation Act, paying HUGE amounts of money to the people who owned enslaved folks, while the newly **_liberated_** people got nothing! Can you imagine being enslaved, then when you are finally free, your former owner gets paid BIG money for "losing their property" and you get zilch? So gross and unfair, right? You're the one who was enslaved! The wildest part? British people were paying for this compensation from their taxes up until 2015!

Here's the thing: reparations and compensation are important, but it is important for the money to go to the people who were harmed, don't you think?

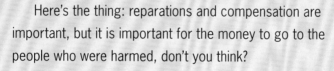

DID YOU KNOW?

While people who were enslaved were not paid reparations, in either the US or the UK, there are several cases of governments or companies making reparations toward groups of people that have been harmed by that country or organization's actions. The best-known instance was established in the 1950s, when Germany rightly set up a reparations program for _Holocaust_ survivors, which continues today.

More recently, in 2005, a declaration adopted by the UN General Assembly stated the "right to benefit from remedies and reparation" for victims of gross human rights violations.

With existing reparations programs in place and a statement from an international body acknowledging victims' rights to compensation, sounds to me like it's time a lot more folks get what they're owed.

CHAPTER 4

WHAT IS THE DIFFERENCE BETWEEN MY "RACE," "NATIONALITY," AND "ETHNICITY"?

It can get a bit confusing, can't it? People use these different categories to describe themselves, and each other, all the time, but "race," "**ethnicity**," and "**nationality**" all have different meanings.

That's partly why when people ask me, "Where are you from, Yassmin?" I don't really know what they are referring to! And between you and me, my answer changes depending on who is asking.

RACE

Hopefully by now you know that "race" was invented by powerful Europeans when they started categorizing people in the same way that they grouped plants and animals. The categories for "race" change depending on where you are in the world, and some places have lots of different categories. One of the main differences between "race" and the other categories like ethnicity is that "race" is often the way in which other people label communities, rather than what those communities choose themselves. However, many people today strongly identify with their racial group and use language to show pride in and _solidarity_ with their community. It really depends on the individual and their history!

NATIONALITY

"Nationality" often refers to the nation that you are a citizen of, the one that can give you a passport. I have two passports, a Sudanese one and an Australian one, which means I have two nationalities: Sudanese and Australian. Depending on the country, your nationality could be decided by where you were born, what passports your parents have, or where you have lived for long enough to be eligible for _citizenship_.

ETHNICITY

Ethnicity is related to your family's history and culture. What are your family traditions, rituals, and histories? What language does your family speak? What did your ancestors speak? This concept includes all the ideas, customs, and behaviors of a group. Different ethnic groups can have different cultures, and these cultures constantly evolve. Some examples of ethnicities can include Tamil, Han Chinese, Slavic, and Nubian. I'm culturally and ethnically Sudanese, but I have also been influenced by the Australian culture that I grew up in and the London culture that I now live in. How wonderful!

DID YOU KNOW?

Definitions of "race" can change depending on the context. I've lived in and traveled to many different countries, and being "Black" has a slightly different meaning in every single place.

In Sudan, we don't often call people Black; we refer more to the shade of people's skin color. (I am usually referred to as "red"!) In France, I am sometimes considered Black and sometimes not, because I have lighter skin—in fact, many have considered me métisse, which means "of mixed racial heritage." In Australia, I am sometimes referred to as brown and sometimes referred to as Black, depending on who I am speaking to.

I have to be considerate, though, because in Australia "Blak" (often without the "c") means First Nations or Indigenous people. When people want to refer to both First Nations people and people of African descent in Australia, they write "Bla(c)k."

Even the idea of who is "white" changes. Decades ago in Australia, Italians and Greeks were not considered "white," but now sometimes they are.

For me, when people want to know about my identity, there is a lot I can say. I can say I am Black, Sudanese, and someone of African descent. I have lighter skin than some of my cousins, and darker skin than others. I am an Australian citizen, a British resident, and a double _**immigrant**_. I speak English and Arabic, and I am getting pretty good at French.

I am what some consider a "third culture kid," someone who has grown up between cultures. Where do I belong? I say I belong to the **_diaspora_**. I can find belonging wherever I am in the world, and that is a wonderful thing. Alhamdulillah.

"Alhamdulillah" is an Arabic word meaning "Thanks be to God" or "Praise God," and it's used by Muslims as well as non-Muslim Arabic speakers around the world.

WHAT NATIONALITY ARE YOU? DO YOU FEEL LIKE YOU BELONG TO YOUR NATIONALITY? WHY OR WHY NOT?

WHAT ETHNIC GROUP ARE YOU? IF YOU DON'T KNOW, MAYBE YOU CAN ASK YOUR PARENTS?

PAIR UP WITH A FRIEND FROM A DIFFERENT ETHNIC GROUP. WRITE THREE THINGS YOU EACH LIKE A LOT ABOUT YOUR ETHNICITY. REMEMBER TO BE KIND AND GENEROUS! NOW DISCUSS.

Whatever your opinion, for me, it's simple: it doesn't really matter what "race," nationality, or ethnicity you are. What matters is whether you are willing to stand up and speak out against racism and racial injustice. We need people of all "races," nationalities, and ethnicities in the fight. No one group can do it alone.

The categories of "race" in a certain place are influenced by its history. It's always best to be guided by the local communities rather than come from the outside and think you have the answer.

IS PREJUDICE THE SAME AS RACISM?

CHAPTER 5

WHAT IS PREJUDICE, YASSMIN?

Before I get into that, I should explain another word: **_bias_**. What is bias? Well, let's look at bias when it comes to pets. Even if you have never had any pets, you might think (based on shows, books, and rumor) that dogs are really friendly and cats are very unfriendly. So when your best friend says they have a new pet cat, you might automatically think *unfriendly*, even though you have never met that cat before! That assumption is biased; it's a shortcut your brain makes. Some biases are helpful (like when we see the color red, our brain thinks *Danger!*), but some biases are based on wrong information. (Like, are all cats unfriendly really? No!) Worse still, some biases can have harmful impacts on other people.

What is a shortcut your brain makes? Brainstorm two or three. Where did you learn these shortcuts? Do you think they're true, or are they based on an unfair bias?

So going back to prejudice. Prejudice is a negative opinion about someone or group of people based on a biased assumption. Racial prejudice is when you are biased against someone based on the "race" you think they are.

If I am biased against a white English man because he is white, that would be considered racial prejudice.

But before you get carried away, wait! Racial prejudice is not the same as racism. Why? Well, a useful shortcut for the explanation is this:

racism = prejudice + power

If you're white, it might hurt if someone is mean about your skin color. It might feel unfair and unkind. And you are right! It is unfair and unkind, and hurting and bullying people isn't right. But before we move on, remember that jetpack?

It's important to remember that all types of prejudice are unfair and hurtful. If we want a fair and just society, we should commit to tackling all our prejudices, as well as fighting racism.

Because of the **_systemic_** advantage a white person has, and because they get to benefit from being part of the dominant culture and centuries of **_oppression_**, they can still—_whoosh!_—zoom up that mountain with their jetpack. If you are white, your "race" isn't going to hold you back. Your feelings may get hurt, but it won't impact your jetpack. That's how power works.

On the other hand, a white person being racist to a Black person has much more impact. Not only does it hurt my feelings, but every racist word or act puts more lead in my shoes, pushing me farther back down the mountain. If a person is in the dominant culture (i.e., if they are white in the US), they have the power of history behind them. Another way to think of it is like this: when a white person does something racist or turns away from helping when I am experiencing racism, it's more than just one moment of sadness. It's like I am being bombed or struck or smashed by everything that's happened before. I am reminded of how powerful white people killed my ancestors, told us lies about ourselves, stole our land and continue to do so, all for their own gain. I reflect on how even though it was the powerful white people who started it off, many of the other white people didn't stop it. They just shrugged and said, "Yeah, whatever." And filled their jetpacks with more blood, sweat, and tears from people like me. Then zoomed off.

SMASHED

STRUCK

BOMBED

Even if I wasn't aware of racism, and didn't know the history or what all the words meant, that doesn't protect me from the impact of it. Whether I see it or not, it's still watering the roots of the racism tree. Growing up, I didn't know much about racism and why it happened, so I didn't have the knowledge to understand when something was a result of racism or not. Most of the time, I blamed myself; I thought things were my fault and wondered whether there was something wrong with me. Looking back, with the knowledge that I now have, I can see the impact of racism in my life. It didn't stop me from doing wonderful things, but it definitely made it a lot harder than if I had been a white North American, a white European, or a white Australian.

In the US, UK, and Australia, my being hurt by a white person's prejudice isn't just about my feelings. I am on the receiving end of a system of oppression that still continues today. It's got the force of power behind it. But it doesn't have to be this way. Human beings created racism, and human beings can get rid of it.

That's why it's so important for all of us to be aware of how we treat each other and also how we support each other when faced with the sneakier racism inside institutions.

How does this section make you feel? Do you understand the difference between racial prejudice and racism?

REMEMBER: TO CHANGE THE SYSTEM, WE ALL NEED TO STAND UP AND SPEAK OUT!

GET RID OF RACISM!

CHAPTER 6

WHAT ABOUT DISCRIMINATION TOWARD RELIGIOUS GROUPS?

Very good question, friend. In order to answer this, first we have to define an important word: "racialization." Remember when I explained that "race" wasn't a biological reality but a social invention that the dominant culture used to control other groups? Well, sometimes that happens with groups that are connected not by skin color or body features but by something else. For example, Muslims in countries like the US and UK are racialized. We get treated like a single "race," as if all Muslims are the same, despite there being almost two billion Muslims in the world! Not only that, but the dominant culture then says, "Muslim people are different from us, and because we think we are better, we are going to push them down." It's a very sneaky trick . . . Someone being different in any way is never a reason to push them down.

There is a term for the prejudice + power that Muslims face. It's called *Islamophobia*. Remember that racism is about power, money, and control. People who benefit from racism will want to distract you by focusing on the technicalities, but don't take your eye off the ball. Focus on justice for all!

Do you understand what racialization means now? If someone says to you that Islamophobia is OK because it "isn't racism," what will you say to them?

Antisemitism

Antisemitism is prejudice against or hatred of Jewish people. It is considered a form of racism, but it is a different type of racism from what we have discussed so far.

Sadly, antisemitism has been around a very long time. Sometimes called "the longest hatred," it has roots—as slavery does—that lie in the pursuit of power and control. Many Christian church leaders wrongly taught that all Jewish people were to blame for the crucifixion of Christ (a lie that they continued to teach for many years) and spread many false myths and rumors about Jewish people, angry that they didn't want to convert to Christianity.

Jewish people were often depicted as "other" and blamed by leaders for anything bad that was happening. Christian European leaders violently excluded Jewish communities economically, socially, and legally. In much of Europe, Jewish people were not allowed to do certain jobs or own land.

Hundreds of years of poisonous antisemitic seeds being planted across Europe laid the groundwork for the Nazis, who believed Jewish people were a so-called separate and dangerous "race" that couldn't be assimilated into society. This led to the horrific Holocaust (also known as the **_Shoah_**): the **_genocide_** of millions of people, including six million Jewish people. During the Second World War, around two out of every three Jewish people living in Europe were killed.

The Nazis used a type of "scientific" racism called **_eugenics_** as part of the justification for their horrific acts. Similar so-called scientific beliefs played a significant role in slavery and have made racism part of our institutions until today.

A lot has been written about the era of the Shoah and anti-semitism today. I would encourage you to read and watch work created by Jewish people on this subject, because as I've said before, it is always best to start with the people who are impacted. One thing that is important to understand, though, is that a key part of the Nazi justification (as they saw it) for the Shoah was the dangerous ideas they had around "race." They believed that people belonged to different "races," and that some were superior to others. So what do we learn here? Racist ideas, stories, and **_stereotypes_** might not appear dangerous at first, but they lay the foundation for terrible violence. We should always be vigilant and ready to stand up and speak out!

HAVE YOU HEARD...?

In 1290, King Edward I of England decided to expel all the Jewish people from what was then the "Kingdom of England." Things had been getting tougher for the Jewish community for a while, but in 1290 they were all pushed out, and they weren't allowed back in until the mid-1650s. Pretty grim, eh?

RACISM
TODAY

OK, I GET WHERE RACISM AND WHITE SUPREMACY COME FROM NOW, BUT THAT WAS SO LONG AGO! WHAT IMPACT DOES IT HAVE TODAY?

WHY, I AM SO GLAD YOU ASKED ... LET'S TAKE A QUICK MOMENT TO RECAP.

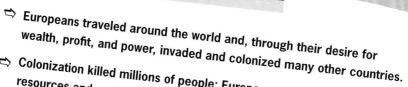

⇨ Europeans traveled around the world and, through their desire for wealth, profit, and power, invaded and colonized many other countries.

⇨ Colonization killed millions of people; Europeans stole land and resources and enslaved many millions of people, kidnapping them and forcing them to work under awful conditions—often until their deaths.

⇨ One of the ways they justified the terrible things they were doing was by creating the idea of "racial" groups, putting that hierarchy into law, and spreading lies that some racial groups were better than others.

⇨ This lie—the lie of white supremacy—has never really disappeared. Today we still live with its impact and the legacy of European colonialism. The curriculum in many imperialist countries teaches that they were mighty and powerful but doesn't question how violently they seized that power or how it was maintained.

As we know, most of the colonizing European countries never said sorry, paid any money back, or changed any of their imperialist systems. They just pretended it didn't really happen or wasn't really that bad. It's a bit of a joke. A sad, murderous, heartbreaking joke . . . and one that many of us who have been hurt by it cannot forget.

It's not so easy to move past hundreds of years of colonization and slavery, especially when the imperialist systems haven't changed. If you look a little more closely at the way the world is today, you will see there is still a lot of work to be done . . . but in order to understand what we need to do, we must truly understand the different ways that racism shows up. It's very adaptable, this racism business. It's good at hiding itself in lots of corners, in places you wouldn't expect. But I'm going to give you some nifty white supremacy–detecting glasses so you can see racism when it rears its dangerous head.

REMEMBER

Many of these outcomes aren't necessarily due to people taking obviously racist actions, although that still does happen. They are also due to our society being based on—rooted in—white supremacy.

white supremacy,

↓ which
leads to

racial injustice (people being treated differently because of the racial group they are in),

↓ which
leads to

unfairness and injustice

CHAPTER 7

HOW DOES RACISM WORK?

Most of the time, we only think of racism as yelling mean words at someone or people like the Ku Klux Klan (the folks with pointy white hats) or hurtful graffiti scrawled on the walls of a house or school. We know it's bad and racist to make fun of people because of their skin color. But racism is a little trickier than that.

Racism is the idea that some "races" are better than others, and white supremacy—which places white people at the top of the racial groups—infects every part of society. It has been made to seem normal, but it is not. We need to learn to be able to spot the ways racism manifests so that we can stand up, speak out, and fight against it.

THERE ARE FOUR KEY WAYS THAT RACISM SHOWS ITSELF:

INTERNALIZED
(inside us)

INTERPERSONAL
(between people)

INSTITUTIONAL
(rules in school
and government)

SYSTEMIC
(how it all comes
together)

INTERNALIZED

When you wish you looked different.

OH, I WISH I HAD STRAIGHT BLOND HAIR LIKE THE GIRLS ON TV!

INTERPERSONAL

When people touch your hair without permission. (A person is not a dog to be petted!)

OMG! I LOVE YOUR HAIR—IT'S SO FLUFFY!

INSTITUTIONAL

When the school dress code doesn't allow for different hairstyles—like braids—that work best with your type of hair.

SYSTEMIC

When you are told to fit in by changing your appearance . . .

WE LIKE OUR STAFF TO LOOK MORE PROFESSIONAL.

but the world is not set up to help people who look like you.

INTERNALIZED (inside us)

When we feel like we are less or more than others because of our "race," or skin color, or hair, or body shape, it is because we have absorbed all the ideas of a racist system into our brains, like a sponge soaking up water. Remember, we are not treated equally, but we are all equally important. Who you are should be celebrated . . . but not at the expense of others.

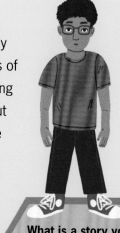

I know that, for a long time, I didn't think I could be beautiful, because I had **_internalized_** the racist idea that white women of European ancestry were the best-looking people in the world. It was in the movies I watched, the advertising everywhere, even in the books I read. I thought—I believed!—that to be beautiful, I had to be skinny and white, with a flat bottom and pointy nose and long, straight, blond hair.

What is a story you believe about people like you? Where does it come from? Do you think it is true? Is this story helping or harming you? What story would make you happier?

Of course, that's not true.
All different types of bodies
are beautiful, obviously.
But I had to work on
my internalized racism and
change the story that I told myself.
Thankfully, I know now I'm *ahem*
actually a babe, if I do say so myself.
Thank you, Allah, for the beautiful body
I was blessed with!

ALSO...

We can have
internalized
beliefs about
other people
and other "races."
We may not say
anything, but we might
have low-key biases about
other racial groups that are a
reflection of white supremacy
and are not actually true. If
you ever find yourself assuming
something about someone because of
their racial group, it's always useful to ask
yourself: *Is that really true? Have I double-
checked? Why do I think this? Where did I
learn that? Can you unpack that belief and
see how it would harm others?*

INTERPERSONAL (between people)

This is what you are probably most familiar with. **_Interpersonal_** racism is when someone does or says something negative about another because of their "race." Typically, this is when someone (usually the one with more power) actively expresses prejudice toward another group of people because of their "race," or because they have absorbed the racist ideas of other people.

Interpersonal racism can take many different forms: straight-out name-calling, using racial **_slurs_**, so-called jokes that make fun of people's perceived racial differences, assumptions that just because someone belongs to a particular group they are naturally better at something or have a particular personality trait, mistaking someone for someone else just because they have the same skin color, loudly making statements about someone's physical features because they are different from the dominant culture, and so much more.

EYE ROLL

WHISPER

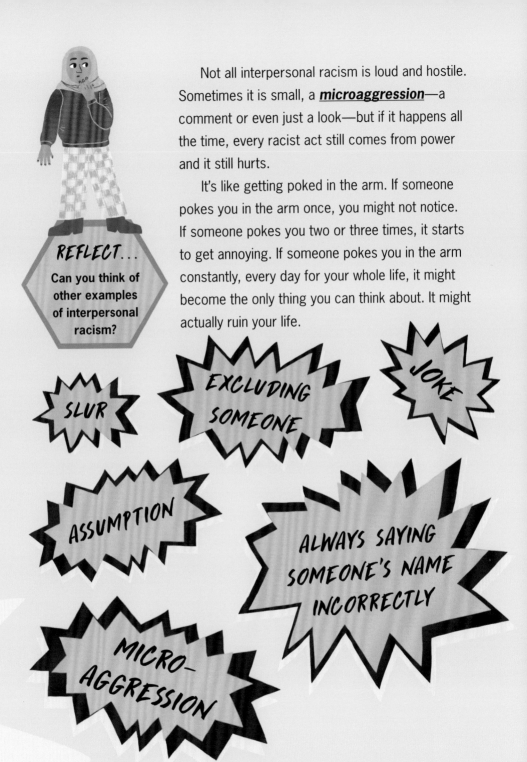

Not all interpersonal racism is loud and hostile. Sometimes it is small, a **_microaggression_**—a comment or even just a look—but if it happens all the time, every racist act still comes from power and it still hurts.

It's like getting poked in the arm. If someone pokes you in the arm once, you might not notice. If someone pokes you two or three times, it starts to get annoying. If someone pokes you in the arm constantly, every day for your whole life, it might become the only thing you can think about. It might actually ruin your life.

REFLECT...

Can you think of other examples of interpersonal racism?

SLUR

EXCLUDING SOMEONE

JOKE

ASSUMPTION

ALWAYS SAYING SOMEONE'S NAME INCORRECTLY

MICRO-AGGRESSION

INSTITUTIONAL

Racism doesn't just exist between people or inside the stories we tell ourselves. It exists in **_institutions_** as well.

WHAT IS AN INSTITUTION?

An institution is a social structure that humans operate within. It can be big, like the government or the education or health systems, or smaller, like a school or a hospital. An institution doesn't stop existing when one person leaves or joins, but it is influenced by those in it and the decisions and choices they make. Often, the history of an institution and how it started can tell us a lot about how it operates today.

You saw on page 51 how someone's hair can affect how they are treated. Let's unpack that a little. Institutions can have formal rules and informal norms. Even if a rule or norm doesn't appear to favor one group of people, the racism becomes clear when you read between the lines. For example, your school could say that the appropriate hairstyle is a "neat ponytail." Many Black people (like me!) have kinky, Afro-textured hair—even if I could get it into a ponytail, to those who set the rules, it might be seen as "messy" or "not appropriate."

> THESE ARE ALL FABULOUS HAIRSTYLES, RIGHT? I PERSONALLY THINK THEY ARE ALL APPROPRIATE.

It's kind of unfair both ways, right? If I do straighten my hair to look "chic," I am disadvantaged compared to my peers because it costs a lot more money, requires more maintenance, and takes up lots of time. If I don't straighten my hair or if I wear a hijab, I am just seen as scruffy and maybe even "inappropriate." By taking white standards of beauty and applying them to everyone, Black people—or anyone whose hair is very different from these standards—are sent the message that we must change something that occurs naturally to us. It's like telling someone to change their eye color.

It is not just the written-down rules either. It's also what we call norms, the unspoken rules or even implicit biases. Sometimes people excuse this by saying, "That's just the way things are." But of course we know that it doesn't have to stay like that. The way things are can be changed—and we are the ones who are going to change it, right?

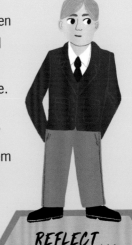

REFLECT...
Do you have a dress code at your school? Does it discriminate unfairly against some types of bodies or hair? If it does, perhaps you can write a letter to your principal explaining why it needs to change!

HAVE YOU HEARD ...?

In 2004, the French government banned religious symbols in schools, meaning that Muslim girls were no longer allowed to wear a hijab to a state-run school. One year after the ban was put in place, about forty to fifty young Muslim girls were expelled because they refused to take off their hijabs. This is a clear example of how a "racialized" group of people, Muslims, can be targeted by rules and policies.

THE HOUSES OF PARLIAMENT

The UK is governed by two Houses of Parliament: the House of Commons and the House of Lords. Both Houses are responsible for passing laws and discussing policies.

In a general election in the UK, citizens over eighteen can vote for the member of Parliament (MP) they'd like to represent their area. The MP who has the most votes is given one of 650 seats in the House of Commons. After the general election in 2019, 10 percent of the MPs in the House of Commons came from outside the dominant culture. But in 2022, out of almost 800 members of the House of Lords, that figure was about 7.3 percent.

Why might there be a higher percentage of white MPs in the House of Lords compared to the House of Commons?

Answer: maybe it has something to do with a history of institutional racism . . .

Unlike in the House of Commons, no one votes on who gets a seat in the House of Lords. Church of England archbishops and bishops take up 24 seats, and 86 other seats are hereditary. Those members inherited the position by being born into an elite family who ruled the UK back in the day (many of which benefited from slavery). All the other members have been picked by the reigning monarch and the prime minister, with some having been recommended

An official 2020 government survey (a census) calculated the percentage of people of color in the US to be 38 percent. Even though Congress has been growing increasingly diverse, and the House of Representatives has proportional representation of some "racial" groups, they have a ways to go before they truly represent the country!

for consideration by a committee. In the House of Lords, you have a seat for life. It can make the process of change very slow.

This is an example of a process that people excuse with "Oh, this is just how it works." Except: it doesn't have to. If they wanted, the members of the House of Lords could change the way seats are awarded. Members of the US Congress could make a difference in America by passing term limits. But that would mean giving up power . . . and not everyone likes to do that.

Remember that institutional racism doesn't mean no Black person or Asian person will ever make it to the top. It just means that their "race" makes it very, very, VERY difficult for them to do so because the world—and this institution in particular—wasn't built with them in mind. In fact, it was built to exclude them. Plus, a handful of people getting to the top doesn't mean things are better or easier for anyone else. The mountain is still there, some people still have jetpacks, and many others still have lead in their backpacks.

Think of your school like the government. Does your community have a school board or school committee? How does someone get selected to serve on it?

SYSTEMIC

A system is a network made up of lots of interconnected parts. Let's lead with an example that's easy to follow: climate change. We are living in a society made up of systems that negatively impact the climate.

No single person is responsible for global warming . . .

but every action contributes to the system.

Some actions are small, like not recycling.

Some actions are big, like large corporations burning fuel.

Some people have more responsibility than others (like those who run countries or big businesses) . . .

but we all have to do our part.

Racism is the same.

Each and every one of us must stand up and speak out against racism, even if we're not directly responsible for it being around. Otherwise, nothing will change.

If you live in a country with racist systems—like we have in Australia, in the UK, and in the US—then it can affect everything: institutions, relationships between people, and people's internal stories. Even if you don't think *you* are racist, the truth is you are either benefiting from or being impacted by racist systems.

WHAT! I'M A GOOD PERSON. WHAT ARE YOU SAYING?

RACISM IN SOCIETY ISN'T ABOUT SAYING AN INDIVIDUAL IS GOOD OR BAD. EVEN IF A PERSON IS NOT ACTIVELY RACIST, THEY WILL STILL BE IMPACTED BY THE RACIST SYSTEM IN WHICH THEY LIVE.

If you look at the top businesspeople in the US, they are almost all white. One of the reasons for this is systemic racism.

But how? you might be wondering. Does this mean that every single person in all those companies is being actively racist?

Well, not quite. Let's break it down.

If you're going to get to the top level of a US business, you need to first get a job in one of those companies, right?

To get a job in a big, prestigious company, you might need one or more of the following:

IN FACT

In 2021, there were only four Black people in the top positions out of the five hundred biggest companies in the US.

- a college degree, preferably from a fancy university
- some work experience at similar companies
- enough money to pay for college, as well as for rent and food when you move out on your own
- a dollop of self-confidence
- maybe some support from your family or other adults in your life
- a lot of luck in the interviewing process

BUT ALL THOSE THINGS ARE NOT EQUALLY ACCESSIBLE TO EVERYONE.

Imagine you live in a neighborhood without great access to public transportation. You get an internship in the city, but both your parents work, so they can't take you. You don't get paid, so you can't afford transportation. That missed opportunity knocks your chances of getting a job down a few pegs.

At school, the teachers don't encourage you to dream big. They just think of you as the class clown. (You might be disrupting class because you've done the schoolwork quicker than everyone else! Or maybe you would have tried harder if someone had encouraged you.) When college applications come around, no one suggests you apply to an Ivy League college. No one helps you or explains the process. They assume you aren't interested or smart enough, even though you would have loved the chance.

Say you do get into college. Many of the other students have parents who went to college and can support them or give advice. Some might have money sent to them so they don't have to work to pay for food or rent. Instead, you have to spend your free time working to earn money, and you don't get enough time to focus on studying, so you end up with lower grades than maybe you know you can get.

Even if you do graduate with decent grades, you need a job. You start applying for positions, lots of them, but people look at your name and maybe can't even pronounce it, or they think, *I'm not sure this person would fit in.* You have a great résumé, but you didn't go to a well-known school or college. Instead, the interviewer picks someone who went to the same prep school as them, or the same college. And so, despite all your hard work, after your hustle at school, at college, working hard to show how good you are, you keep getting rejected. You might start to think it's your fault, until one day, your interviewer pronounces your name correctly, knows the neighborhood you are from, asks about your family. That's when you get the job.

It takes a long time to undo hundreds of years of injustice and **inequality**, based on slavery, colonization, racism, and wealth, because the roots go so deep. Just as you may think you've gotten rid of a tree once you've chopped it down, it's not really gone if you have forgotten to take out the deep, deep roots.

We must take responsibility for our individual actions, but it's more than just that. We need to fight all the levels of racism in order to make society better for us all: make the rules fair, stop racism between people, and change the way we think about ourselves.

The only way we can make change is to all work together.

WHAT ARE YOU GOING TO DO ABOUT RACISM? STAND UP AND SPEAK OUT!

CHAPTER 8

WHAT DOES RACISM LOOK LIKE TODAY?

Racism and white supremacy are very adaptable forces that act like shape-shifters. But remember, even though racism may take different forms, the same racial injustice is at the core. In this section, we will learn how to pick out the shape-shifting forms of today.

HISTORY DOESN'T HAVE TO KEEP REPEATING!

The systemic stuff feeds into the institutional, trickles down into the interpersonal, and fertilizes the internal.

↓

It becomes a self-fulfilling prophecy, a sad cycle that won't change... UNLESS we interrupt it and, in doing so, change the world.

↓

To interrupt the cycle, you've got to learn how to spot it...

Education and law enforcement are two structures that have a big impact on everyday life: every child has to receive an education, and the police force has authority over everyone in the country. In a just and safe society, we would hope that schools and the police force treat everyone fairly, right?

But we're not quite there yet. Once you know how to spot racism and you start looking more closely at these institutions, you can identify the injustice baked into all these structures.

To do this, you need to think about the following:

1. *The way these institutions were set up, who they were intended to serve, and why.*

2. *How that affects the way racist attitudes are passed down.*

3. *How these attitudes play out in places like the classroom, the streets, the newspapers, or on TV.*

**READY?
LET'S GO...**

SCHOOLS

In the United States, almost 80 percent of teachers are white. And even if teachers of color are represented in schools, the big bosses are almost always white (in a 2017–2018 survey, the National Center for Education Statistics reported that white principals were the majority in every state except Hawai'i). While a classroom might be full of students from a wide range of different backgrounds, the person teaching the classroom, deciding grades, and running the school is more often than not going to be someone from the dominant culture—white. If every teacher comes from a similar background in the dominant culture, they are less likely to recognize racist structures or understand the range of experiences that are lived by their students.

Do most of your teachers look like you? Your principal? How does this affect your cultural and community connections within the school?

WHAT EFFECT CAN THIS STRUCTURE HAVE ON THE STUDENTS?

The problem goes deeper still. Having leaders from the dominant culture, who must teach a curriculum full of biases and stereotypes (because of the country's history), can lead to interpersonal racism when teachers aren't aware of their own assumptions. If the teachers in a school constantly reinforce negative stereotypes, the kids they teach absorb that story, leading to internalized racism!

Schools are an important part of society. Sadly they often reflect the racist attitudes of the day. In the US, it took until 1954 for the Supreme Court to desegregate schools, and much longer for states to willingly participate.

Unfortunately, this kind of racist grouping and stereotyping continues today. According to a survey of more than five hundred people that was conducted by the YMCA in 2020, young Black people in the UK believe they're seen as the "class clown" or an "underachiever" or they are assumed to be "less capable," "unintelligent," and "aggressive."

Furthermore, 50 percent of those young Black people believe teachers' perceptions of them are one of the biggest barriers to their achievement in school. Imagine how you might feel if, just because you're curious and you ask lots of questions, the teacher assumes you're "disruptive" and treats you differently because of it. They have made their mind up based on their bias about Black people, not on your behavior, but it means they don't take your questions seriously or give you positive encouragement. If you do well on a test, they act surprised! How insulting is that? If this happens enough times . . . you might absorb the message, right?

This isn't to say you shouldn't make jokes (I was definitely that kid who talked way too much in class), but know that sometimes a teacher's opinion is more about their bias than about your potential.

POLICE

The police force is an institution that has power over the whole community. This includes the authority to use force to keep control of people and enforce the law. The police say their purpose is to protect, but it's worth asking, Who are the police protecting, and from whom? Around the world, police forces have often been set up to protect only people in the dominant culture—in the US, for example, the police was established to support the wealthy, white slave owners.

In the US and UK, Black people are more likely to be stopped and searched by the police than white people are. In the case of sentencing for crimes (whether you go to jail and for how long), you are more likely to be sent to prison for the same crime if you are Black or brown than if you are white. This doesn't seem fair, does it?

What's even more unfair is the way sentencing is reported. In the UK, a 2019 study* showed that the Met Police (the police force of London) did not report all sentences in the same way to the press. They were much more likely to mention the ethnicity of the person in the press release *if that person was Black.*

So police aren't just being unfair in how they treat Black and brown people— they are responsible for shaping how the public thinks of those people by using something called **_selective reporting_**.

THE DAILY

SENSATIONAL HEADLINE!

Something
happened,
but instead
of presenting
all the information, we're
going to report it in a
specific and unfair way!

THE 📖 NEWS

FIGURES FROM JULY 2019–DECEMBER 2019: UK MINISTRY OF JUSTICE AND HUFFPOST UK RESEARCH

CITY STORIES

WHY AM I ALWAYS IN TROUBLE?

HAHA! I GOT AWAY WITH IT!

Imagine you had two siblings: a brother and a sister. The sister stole money from you every week, and the brother stole from you every month. But you only told your parents when your brother stole from you. Your parents are going to assume that your brother is the really naughty one, right? Even though that's not really what is going on! By presenting the information a certain way, it looks like more Black people are committing violent crimes, even though that's not true. Reporting information with a racial bias like this affects the way people think about Black people, not just when they worry about crime but also more generally. This is one of the ways internal biases against Black people are fed on a daily basis. These are just a few examples of how racism can impact the lives of Black people. We haven't even touched on how racism impacts the lives of people from every other racial group! It's wild, and tragic. Racism makes so many of our lives worse. It turns things that should be fun or important, like school or hanging out with friends, into difficult—maybe even dangerous—activities. I often wonder how much easier my life would be without having to deal with racism. This stuff wears you down! It's exhausting. It hurts, and sometimes it kills. We've gotta work together to get rid of it.

CHAPTER 9

WHY DOES REPRESENTATION MATTER?

YOU CAN'T BE WHAT YOU CAN'T SEE.

Sometimes it can be hard to imagine what the future will look like, what we can be when we grow up. So we look to adults for inspiration! But what if all the people you see in certain roles are from the dominant culture? Like, if you're Black but see only white models on catwalks, or if you're a woman or nonbinary and see only cisgender male astronauts. Not seeing yourself reflected can make you think there's no room for people like you in the places you want to go . . .

Do you have very curly hair? Me too. You know, Black curly hair is like magic! It can do all sorts of different things and be put into styles that no other hair in the world can. Back in the day, women used to braid secret messages into their hair, finding undercover ways to communicate. Our hair has the power of centuries of strong ancestors, and it's something to be proud of.

I'm going to let you in on a little secret. You see, for a long time, I wasn't super proud of my hair. I didn't know the wonderful history of Afro-textured hair, people made fun of it, and I didn't see that many powerful people in the world with hair like mine. No one on TV, in Parliament, in advertising, or in books looked like me.

It wasn't just about hair either. There was no representation of people like me—a woman who is Black, muscly, and Muslim—and it made me feel invisible. To make matters worse, if there ever were people like me on TV or in the news, they were never presented in a positive light.

Everyone should have the opportunity to see people who look like them in all walks of life: in sports, politics, business, art, even just in the background in scenes on TV! Seeing yourself is powerful. Telling our own stories is even better! That's why I write books about people like me—*You Must Be Layla* and *Listen, Layla*. I want to bring characters from my world into all our worlds; not just flat characters who reflect the harmful biases and stereotypes of society, but wonderful types who are funny and flawed, characters who reflect us as humans.

Whether it's the shape of your nose, your bottom, your head, or your lips. Whether it's how tall or short you are, or how much melanin your skin has, or how your name twists the tongues of those not familiar with it. Your body, name, and language contain the stories of your ancestors and the power and strength that they had. You should be proud of them. The world is wrong to tell you to change. What makes you different is what makes you special.

No one else on this Earth can be you better than you can. Treasure that, and make the absolute most of it.

CHAPTER 10

WHAT IS STEREOTYPING, AND WHY IS IT BAD?

FRENCH PEOPLE LOVE CHEESE.

GIRLS LIKE PINK.

MOM DOES THE COOKING.

BOYS LIKE CARS.

TALL PEOPLE PLAY BASKETBALL.

SHORT HAIR IS FOR BOYS.

A stereotype is a type of belief about a group of people. It is often an oversimplification, sometimes even a lie, like "Boys like football." Thing is, stereotypes often have negative impacts, even when they seem "positive."

How can a positive stereotype have a negative impact? Saying "Asian people are good at math," for example, might seem like a nice thing, but imagine this: if you are good at math, people are going to think it's because you're Asian and not because you have worked super hard, and if you're bad at math, people might make a joke about how unexpected this is "because you're Asian!" So both ways, it's kind of unfair. Plus, because people expect better from you (unfairly!), you might even get graded more harshly.

Stereotypes can be created by selective reporting (as on pages 68–69) and reinforced by the stories we tell. Stereotypes also feed biases, the shortcuts our brains make as we move through the world.

You'll see I've used some stereotypes on previous pages to make a point. Can you go through the book and find them? What do you think the impact of them might be?

Stereotypes aren't just about "race." They exist about every group of people—girls, boys, teachers, people who like science, people who like sports. All stereotypes can be harmful. Racist stereotypes often have a harmful impact in particular because they reinforce the white supremacist hierarchy.

How does this work? Well, if you constantly repeat a stereotype, people are going to start believing it is true, and that acts like fertilizer for all the seeds of racism that have been planted . . . and racist beliefs grow into racist actions.

We might also start to believe those stereotypes ourselves. It's another way that internalized racism takes hold.

How do you think untrue rumors make someone feel? What impact do you think that has on their life?

It's like a rumor at school. Imagine a school bully starts spreading a rumor that you peed your pants. If enough people hear it, share it on social media, and pass it on, people start to believe it, right? Your principal might pull you aside and say, "Excuse me, I heard you peed your pants—is everything OK?" You deny it, but the principal doesn't believe you. From now on, that's what everyone—including the teaching staff—thinks: you're a pants pee-er now! Even though it's not true! Imagine everyone you meet thinking that you might pee your pants.

DID YOU KNOW?

Too often, people in power spread negative stereotypes about Muslim women. One British politician compared people wearing religious face coverings to "letter boxes" (which look like mail slots in the US) or "bank robbers." How insulting is that? Comparing a living, breathing human to an object is dehumanizing. Claiming they look like criminals is offensive and cruel. Another British politician described Muslim women as traditionally submissive, encouraging people to believe we need to be "saved" from our religion, or to tell us that "Muslim women are oppressed." Obviously, that's a big fat lie—I don't need saving; I can make my own decisions, thank you very much.

But a stereotype, a myth, is a negative story that gets told again and again and again and is kept alive by the people who listen to it. The myth then becomes the justification for rules and _policies_ to hurt and control that group of people. It's hard to avoid stereotypes, but we can challenge them when they arise. Pay attention to the stories people with power spread, because sometimes they are doing more harm than good!

Hijabs-R-Us

As you've learned, France (and other countries, such as Belgium) has passed laws that ban Islamic face coverings, and in some institutions, they've even banned the hijab! More recently, the EU followed suit, saying employers are allowed to ban the hijab at work. They get away with this because they claim it will "prevent social disputes" or help Muslim women "free themselves." But you know what actually happens? The opposite. It **stops** Muslim women from going into politics, like when a hijabi woman was banned from a political party because she wore a hijab in her campaign poster. It **stops** women from pursuing sports, because stores don't stock hijabi-friendly clothing. And it even **stops** people from being able to stay in the country. When I was living in France, they rejected my visa because I was wearing a hijab in my photo. If I wanted to stay in France, they said I would have to take it off for the photo. So, because of French laws, I had to leave . . . and France lost out on my brilliance! Pretty terrible, hey? These laws don't help anyone, really. They feed on people's fear, and they make life more difficult for Muslim women.

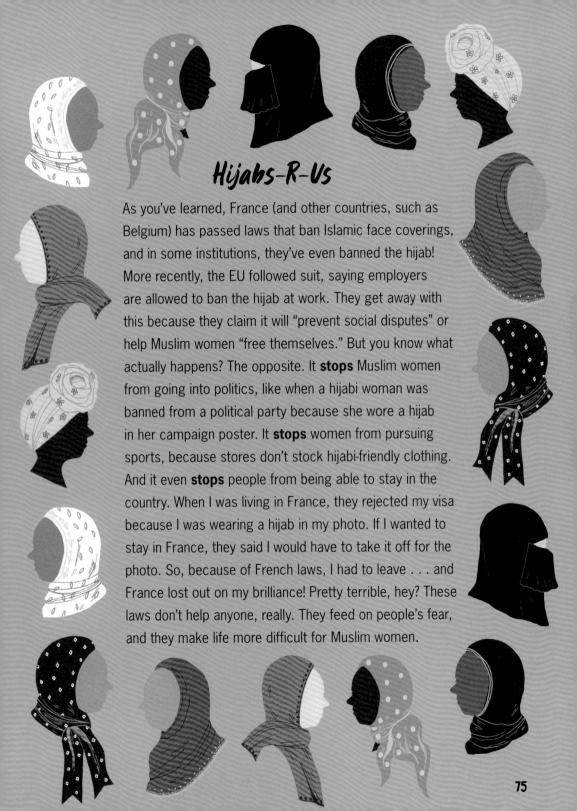

CHAPTER 11

WHAT IS JUSTICE?

We have talked a lot about where racism comes from, how and why it started, and what it looks like today. But now I want us to look forward. What does a world *beyond* white supremacy look like? How do we change things for the better? Right now things are unequal . . .

INEQUALITY

EQUALITY

Some people say they fight for EQUALITY. _Equality_ means everyone gets the same amounts of everything . . . and that might seem like a good idea, but it still doesn't fully get rid of the problem because of all the history, right? If the system is still unfair, equal isn't enough.

EQUITY

Some people say, "OK, then, I will work toward EQUITY!" _Equity_ means giving people the specialized tools they need to get the same opportunities, to make up for the unfair system. That is also a bit better . . . but still not perfect, right? Because of the history of unfairness, the opportunities are still not spread out equally. So . . .

I'M HERE TO HELP YOU WITH FLYING LESSONS . . .

SEE YOU UP THERE!

JUSTICE

I say we work toward JUSTICE. As well as improving equity, justice addresses history and takes apart racist systems, providing everyone with the best tools, opportunities, and resources. Instead of everyone getting jetpacks, why not work together to build a vehicle to take everyone up the mountain? A system and a society that is fair, safe, and just for all!

WITH ALL THE MONEY WE SAVED ON JETPACKS, WE BUILT A CABLE CAR FOR EVERYONE!

MERITOCRACY

Sometimes people say things like, "You just have to work equally as hard and you will be equally rewarded! It's all about merit." Be careful! The idea of merit, or **meritocracy**, is a distraction from the truth. Sometimes, because the system is unjust, working equally as hard will not get you the same recognition as someone from the dominant, elite culture. Don't be distracted by the urge of the powerful to put all the responsibility on the individual. We need to change the system!

HOW TO STAND UP AND SPEAK OUT

OK.
LET'S ALL TAKE A DEEP BREATH.
WOW, LEARNING ABOUT RACISM
CAN BE HEAVY, RIGHT?

HOW TO STAND UP AND SPEAK OUT

I know I get a bit overwhelmed sometimes, taking in all the unfair things that happen in the world. Some adults might think you don't need to know about racism until you are grown up, but I disagree. You are all smart, capable, and intelligent human beings, and injustice affects you too, so it is important that you know about it. Also, between you and me, many adults don't know this stuff that well either! You might have to give this book to the adults you know after you read it so they can learn a thing or two . . .

BUT WAIT, YOU'VE TOLD US ALL ABOUT HOW BAD THINGS ARE. YOU HAVEN'T TOLD US WHAT TO DO ABOUT IT!

YOU'RE TOTALLY RIGHT. NOW THAT YOU KNOW WHAT YOU ARE FIGHTING AGAINST (RACISM IN ALL ITS FORMS) AND WHAT YOU ARE WORKING TOWARD (RACIAL JUSTICE), LET'S LOOK AT SOME REALLY PRACTICAL WAYS WE CAN MAKE THIS HAPPEN.

I know it can be really hard sometimes to talk to adults about important issues like these. I remember when I was a young person, it was always so very frustrating when adults didn't listen to me. However! Don't be discouraged! It is normal for adults to push back when someone—even other adults—challenge the way they think. But what you're doing is really important, and even if people don't seem to be paying attention or changing right away, you might be surprised at how much they're actually taking in.

REMEMBER

You're planting seeds here, wonderful, healthy seeds of positive change. Now practice standing up and speaking out in a safe manner, so when the opportunity comes up, you know just what you need to do.

LOOK BACK

You've seen ideas for things to think about or exercises in boxes throughout this book. Try looking back through the book and picking out ones you think are easy to remember. You could practice saying them out loud to yourself in the mirror to help give you confidence bringing them up. Even if you don't get it right the first time, that's OK. Practice makes perfect, so remember to practice fighting racism!

CHAPTER 12

WHY SHOULD I CARE ABOUT RACISM WHEN THERE ARE SO MANY OTHER THINGS GOING ON?

Sometimes it can feel like there are lots and lots of things to fix in the world, and we don't have enough time or energy to fix them all by ourselves. You might care a lot about the environment and climate change, making things better for people of different genders and sexualities, making your school more accessible for people with disabilities, or helping families who have less money than others. If you do, that's great! All these issues are really important.

The thing is, racism is something that **_intersects_** all of these different topics. Racism means that people of color and those who live in formerly colonized countries are more likely to be exposed to harmful pollution and poor infrastructure. Racism means that if you are a poor Black person, you will probably be treated less kindly by the government than a poor white person. It means that if you are part of the

If you are already involved in fighting for another social justice issue, then are there people who you look up to in that field who are of different "races"? Or are all the people you consider leaders white? Do you follow any Indigenous climate change activists? Any Black anti-poverty campaigners?

LGBTQ+ community, you might have to deal with racism inside the LGBTQ+ community, even though that is supposed to be a safe space.

Whatever social issue a person faces, they deal with racism on top. So even if it isn't the main thing you care about, it's important that we know how to tackle it so that life is better for us all!

FOR US!
BY US!

WHAT DO WE WANT?
SOLIDARITY!
WHEN DO WE WANT IT?
NOW!

LISTEN TO US!

MY VOICE

LET US LEAD!

WE WANT SOLIDARITY!

Imagine you are having a really tough time with your basketball team. You are losing a lot (like, all of the games) and you need to work together to figure things out. Now, if some random person from another school (let's call them Steve)—who has never played basketball before but is very good at tennis—just turned up and started giving you his opinion, would you listen? If he just said all of you were silly and you should listen to his advice, would you pay him any attention at all? Probably not, right? Steve doesn't know what he is talking about! Don't be like Steve. Don't think you know more about someone else's experience. Remember to **listen** and **learn**, but only **lead** if it's your place to do so.

Everyone has a different way of making change in the world. I love leading, but my younger brother, for example, doesn't like being at the front or onstage at all, and that's OK. It is important to allow everyone to find their own path, so remember that you shouldn't pressure anyone to lead, or take charge of making change, unless they want to.

CHAPTER 13

HOW DO YOU UNDO STEREOTYPES?

On pages 72–73, we learned that a stereotype is an idea that people repeat such that others can end up believing it is true. Just like a rumor. Now the question I have for you is . . . how do you fight a rumor?

The reality is that our media is full of stereotypes about people from different ethnicities, cultures, and "races." You may think they are a joke, but quite often stereotypes are a way for racist ideas to sneak, camouflaged, into society. Pay attention to who is pushing what stereotype and why. Are they doing this to lift someone up, or to make fun of them and take power away from them? When you see negative stereotypes, it's important to stand up and speak out.

> Can you think of stereotypes applied to different groups of people portrayed in the media? How do you think that makes them feel? Can you think of a way to challenge these stereotypes?

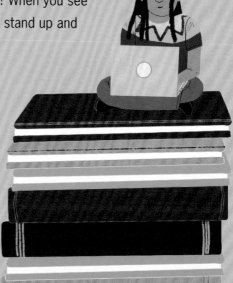

It is vital to see *positive* representations of ourselves out in the world. It plays a key role in helping different groups of people feel important, valued, and part of society. However, remember—it won't bring about systemic change on its own. Representation needs to be combined with power to change society for the better. Without a shift in power, it's like the person with the jetpack wearing lead weights because weights got "cool." Good for them! But that person has more power and the choice to wear what they want. But if the people with lead backpacks can't choose a jetpack—if it doesn't work both ways— what has really changed?

THE POWER OF STORIES

Part of what has happened in history is that we have only really celebrated the achievements of the people in the establishment—elite, powerful white European men. From reading history books, you might think that these were the only people who ever did anything, but of course that is not true. They just spent hundreds of years telling everyone else that only their work was important, interesting, or worth paying attention to. They wrote the history books to make themselves look good. But that's changing. We are writing our own stories now, aren't we?

CHAPTER 14

ALL THE REALLY BAD STUFF HAPPENED SO LONG AGO. I DIDN'T DO IT. WHY SHOULD I CARE? IT'S NOT MY FAULT!

You are right. It's not your fault that we live in a world where racism is everywhere. We can't change what happened in the past. However, we can definitely admit that where we are now is influenced by all the things that happened in the past. And that if we want a world that is safe and fair for everyone, then we should all definitely work together to make that happen.

REMEMBER
I don't want you to feel guilty. You're not responsible for the actions of people in the past. But I do want you to be responsible for how you act today. Feel angry that the world is unfair and excited about working toward racial justice.

WHERE DO I START?

CHAPTER 15

In chapter 7 we talked about the different types of racism: internalized, interpersonal, institutional, and systemic. Each one requires a slightly different approach. The framework I like to use is something called the "Circles of Power."

Look at the image below . . .

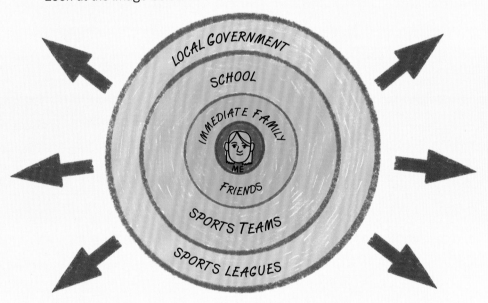

In the first circle is you! This is to remind you that fighting for racial justice can start with what is happening inside you: the internalized racism. As we move out from the center, we enter the areas where you have different levels of influence and power. Next come the interpersonal relationships (between friends and family and people you encounter in the world around you). Then we move to the circle of institutions (your school, sports team, and so on), and then the system in which they exist. Each area will have different methods for tackling racism.

CHAPTER 16

HOW CAN I ADDRESS INTERNALIZED RACISM?

If you, like me, are not part of the dominant culture in the country where you live, I want you to make it your mission to ensure you fight any internalized racism that might sneak its way into your brain. Here are some ways in which I did this . . .

1. *I learned more about the history of where I was born and where my parents came from. I learned that there was so much in the history of Sudanese people to be proud of! Like, did you know that we have more pyramids than Egypt? And that in 400 BCE we used to have many powerful queens, during the time of the Kingdom (or Queendom!) of Kush? It is so important that you are proud of who you are and all that you have come from, especially if you are not in the dominant culture.*

    Finding out more about our past and stories allows us to grow strong, deep roots in fertile ground. It's a connection to the powerful parts of our history that have been hidden from us that can help us weather any storm.

If possible, find out more about your family's cultural or ethnic history. If you aren't currently connected to your family, that's OK! Maybe you can work with someone who is close to you to find out more about the culture of your ancestors or your chosen family.

2. I started reading stories about people who were not part of the dominant culture. For a long time, I only read books with a main character who was part of the dominant culture. I loved those books—don't get me wrong! But they sometimes made me feel invisible. Once I found books, movies, TV shows, and other media that had awesome main characters of different "races" and genders, and who came from different places, I started to feel like I could belong.

If you worry that you have absorbed other people's racist ideas, no matter who you are, you can follow the same steps to undo those harmful thoughts even if they aren't directed inward. Choose to learn about other people's cultures and history by asking them questions or reading books created by someone outside the dominant culture. And don't think that other people should change just to fit in; instead, accept people as they are.

3. Remember that you matter and are wonderful just the way you are. Sometimes you may be in a situation where you feel like you need to change yourself to fit in—whether it is because of the way you look, act, or even smell. But remember: no one else should get to control how you feel about yourself. I will tell you my secret. Whenever I am in a really tough situation, I ask myself this question: If I was a character in a movie right now, what would I do?

Learn to notice whenever a not-nice thought or story creeps into your brain. When you see it coming, imagine another voice in your brain—a kind, loving, caring voice that is going to remind you that you are wonderful, important, valued. Don't let the not-nice voice have any power over you!

CHAPTER 17

INTERPERSONAL:
WHAT SHOULD I DO IF I SEE ACTS OF RACISM HAPPEN IN FRONT OF ME?

If you see obvious racism happening in front of you and don't act, then you are allowing it to happen and sending out the message that, at some level, you think it's OK. But I know it can be scary to get involved, so here are some ways that you can do so safely . . .

SAFETY FIRST!

Before you get involved in any situation, it is always important to do a safety check. What you don't want is for things to escalate. That becomes dangerous for everyone. You want to (1) show the person being targeted you have their back and (2) make it clear to everyone that racism is not OK. Only step in if you feel safe.

If you are part of the dominant culture (in the US, if you are white), it's important to speak out against racism even if there are only white people around and there isn't anyone of a different "race" there to notice. You don't pick up litter only when someone's looking, right?

Here's what you can do if . . .

SOMEONE MAKES A RACIST JOKE.

Instead of laughing, ask them to explain why they think it's funny! Just be like . . .

It will make them feel very awkward, and they might not do that again. Even if they explain, you still don't have to laugh. Racism isn't funny! Instead, explain why this isn't OK.

SOMEONE IS SAYING RACIST THINGS TO ANOTHER PERSON.

Rather than confronting the person who is being racist, start a conversation with the person being targeted. Here are some things you could say:

You can also check in and ask if they are OK.

SOMEONE MAKES A JUDGMENT ABOUT OTHER PEOPLE BECAUSE OF THEIR "RACE."
Rather than telling them they are wrong, ask them questions.

You can also say things like, "Oh, well, I heard this instead . . . What do you think about that?" It's helpful to keep asking questions, because with the right questions you can guide them to see things in a different way.

These are just examples to help get you started; your experience won't be exactly the same. Sometimes it will feel right to speak out directly to someone being racist—sometimes it will be better to focus your support on the person being targeted.

REMEMBER

If you see or hear something racist happening (and you have the power to do something about it), you don't have to wait for the person being attacked to stand up for themselves before you do anything. Check that it is safe, then use your power for good!

THINGS TO REMEMBER!

It's always easier to stand up together. So if you see someone stepping in to challenge a racist saying or action, rather than just letting them deal with it by themselves, why don't you back them up? You might not be comfortable being the first one to speak, but you can definitely be the second, or third, or even fourth person to add your voice to the chorus of support.

If you are the first person to stand up and speak out, you can also look around and encourage people to back you up! Sometimes people need a slight prompt to get involved. Remember: be encouraging, and use questions like, "What do you think?"

WHAT DO YOU THINK?

The aim of stepping in isn't to focus on you; it's to help the person being attacked, and to make it clear that racism is not OK. If the person being targeted asks you to stop, it is important to listen and respect their wishes. It's about them, not you!

CHAPTER 18

HOW CAN I ENCOURAGE OTHERS TO BE ANTI-RACIST, INCLUDING MY PARENTS OR TEACHER?

Like anything that requires some courage, some backbone, some strength of the soul, it's always better to encourage others through our actions as well. It's like when someone tells you to jump into a very, very, very cold pool . . .

If they're asking you to do it first because they are too scared, you're probably not going to do it. If they're already in the pool, you might jump in to join them, but it still might be a bit too scary. The best option is for both of you to jump in together!

If you have a friend, a parent, a teacher, or someone else in your life who you want to jump into the pool with, why don't you ask them to join you on the journey? This can be better than telling them what they are doing wrong and then trying to convince them to get into a very cold pool when you're already in it.

There are lots of ways, big and small, that you can bring others along with you:

1. Show them what you're reading (this book!) and learning about.
2. Ask them what they know, or what they think, to get the discussion going. Conversations about "race" and racial justice are so important.
3. You could ask them how much they know about the history of the United States.
4. Ask them if they know that "race" is not biological but social.
5. Ask them whether they have friends from different "races" or cultures. If not, why not? How do they think they could make friends from different communities?
6. Ask them whether the adults they know work in places that have anti-racism policies, or whether it's something they could discuss.
7. Ask them whether they have ever thought about their biases and assumptions and where those may have come from.
8. Suggest movies and books and TV shows where the main characters are different "races." (Or maybe you can find some shows in different languages too!)

GOOD LUCK!

Who are you going to jump into the pool with? Is there someone you have in mind? Who is your racial justice buddy? Do you have a friend you are reading this book with? Maybe you can tackle these challenges together!

YOU DON'T HAVE TO TACKLE THESE THINGS ALL AT ONCE. THINK ABOUT HOW TO BRING THEM INTO LOTS OF DIFFERENT CONVERSATIONS.

CHAPTER 19

WHAT SHOULD I DO IF SOMEONE IS RACIST TO ME?

The world can be very unfair, and you might think it is your fault someone is being racist, but it's not. Remember that what they are saying is not true. You're as good, as beautiful, as smart, as powerful as everyone else—it's just sad that we live in a world that sometimes doesn't see that.

If someone is being racist, ask yourself these questions:

IS THIS SOMEONE I CARE ABOUT?

NO

Then their opinion of you doesn't matter, and you can ignore them. Continue your day with your head held high!

YES

Then proceed to the next question . . .

IS THIS SOMEONE WHO IS OPEN TO CHANGING THEIR MIND? IS THIS SOMEONE WHO WOULD LISTEN TO YOU IF YOU TOLD THEM THEIR ACTIONS WERE RACIST?

NO

Then you should keep yourself safe, first and foremost! Maybe change the subject and then later tell someone else who you think can help you.

YES

Then give them the feedback sandwich.

COMPLIMENT

THE IMPORTANT INFORMATION

COMPLIMENT

Be specific about the thing that is racist (like touching my hair without asking, using that word, etc.) and then tell the other person how it makes you feel. It's important you focus on how it makes you feel because that way, the other person can't argue back! For example:

I LOVE OUR FRIENDSHIP AND I KNOW YOU CARE ABOUT ME. I JUST WANT TO TELL YOU THAT WHEN YOU TOUCH MY HAIR, IT FEELS LIKE YOU'RE PATTING ME LIKE A DOG, IT MAKES ME FEEL REALLY SMALL AND TERRIBLE, AND YOU DIDN'T EVEN ASK, WHICH WAS KIND OF WEIRD. SO I WOULD APPRECIATE IT IF YOU DIDN'T TOUCH MY HAIR . . . I KNOW YOU'LL LISTEN TO ME BECAUSE YOU'RE A REALLY GOOD FRIEND.

You can also write yourself a little script (or use the example above) and then practice! Practice, practice, practice, because then, in the moment, it will make things much easier to say. As part of your practice, perhaps you could talk it through with someone you trust. There are lots of ways to manage when people are racist toward us. But life is a big old mountain when it comes to racism. Some obstacles are worth tackling, and some are not worth the effort and it's better to walk away. So pick your battles, educate others where you can, and remember: it's not *you*; it's the racist system that we live in.

CHAPTER 20

MY FRIEND SAID I WAS RACIST TO THEM, BUT I DIDN'T MEAN TO BE! HOW CAN I BE RACIST IF I DIDN'T MEAN IT?

Have you ever been called racist? It can be scary, right? Your stomach might drop, your heart might start pumping faster, and the first thing you want to do is shout, "NO! No! No, I'm not! You're wrong!"

Ah, my dear friend. If someone says you are racist, the first thing I want you to do is take a big, deep breath. And another. And another. Make sure they're big, deep belly breaths. Because if we don't, we might start getting defensive. We might get angry because we feel like someone is telling us we are a bad person, and we don't want to be bad, do we?

It's good you have recognized doing racist things is bad. That's a great instinct to have! But for a good instinct to turn into a good action, we have to stop ourselves from reacting defensively and think about how we are going to act positively.

I DON'T WANT TO BE RACIST, SO WHAT DID I DO THAT WAS WRONG?

This is a tough situation to be in, but let's go through it together. If someone says something you did was racist, and you did not realize this at the time, remember that they are not saying that you are a bad person. They are saying something you did was racist. This doesn't make you bad. It means you are a person who has—intentionally or not—done something that played into the wrongful idea that some "races" are better than others.

We all make mistakes. Quite often we might say or do a racist thing without meaning to . . . because racism is everywhere.

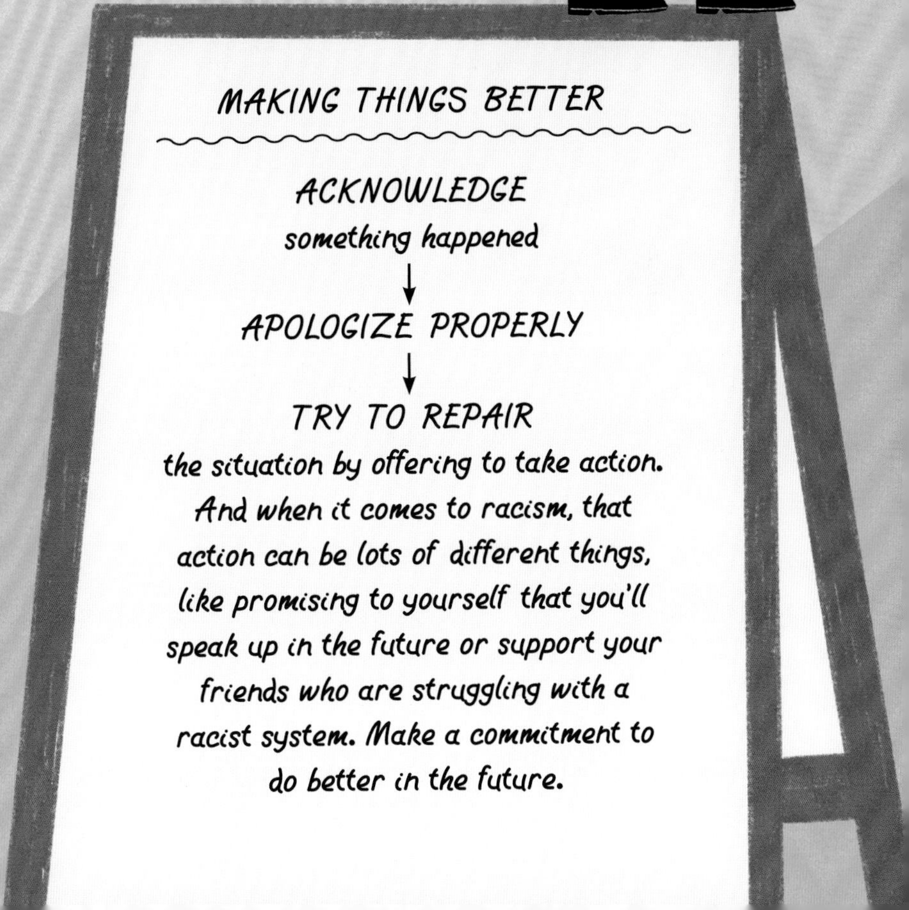

MAKING THINGS BETTER

ACKNOWLEDGE
something happened

↓

APOLOGIZE PROPERLY

↓

TRY TO REPAIR
the situation by offering to take action. And when it comes to racism, that action can be lots of different things, like promising to yourself that you'll speak up in the future or support your friends who are struggling with a racist system. Make a commitment to do better in the future.

Whether or not something is racist isn't about what you *meant* or *intended*. Like, you might be riding your bicycle and accidentally run into someone, hurting their arm. OUCH! Whether you meant to run into them doesn't matter; it happened and you have hurt them. Denying it—or pretending it didn't happen, or getting angry because they said you ran into them—isn't going to change anything.

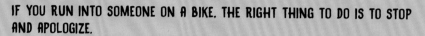

IF YOU RUN INTO SOMEONE ON A BIKE. THE RIGHT THING TO DO IS TO STOP AND APOLOGIZE.

I'M SORRY.

Now, they might be angry, but it's understandable! They are hurt. You might then ask if they're OK.

ARE YOU OK? WHERE DID I HURT YOU?

They might show you where you have hurt their arm. Oh no! Might be time to get some first aid . . . and figure out how to use the brakes on your bike.

It's the same with racism! If someone tells you that something you said or did was racist, the first thing to do is stop—just like you would if you ran into someone with a bike—and check out the damage.

Sometimes when we are told we have done something wrong, we can get . . . defensive. Say, for example, you and your sibling are play-fighting, and then all of a sudden they squeal and scream, "Hey! That hurts!"

What is your reaction?

NO, IT DOESN'T. SHUT UP!

I DON'T THINK SO!

WHAT HURTS?

OH, SORRY I HURT YOU!

YOU HURT ME FIRST!

Some of these responses are defensive. They either deny your sibling's pain or try to make an excuse for it. But you and I both know that denying or making excuses for harmful behavior isn't really right. We are our best selves when we are kind and generous and admit that we have hurt someone and are sorry for it, no matter how hard that is! And I know it's hard! But we all make mistakes and sometimes cause harm to other people, intentionally or unintentionally. The important thing to remember is that when this happens, we should use it as an opportunity to learn, and not be scared! Just say sorry and try your best not to do it again.

CHAPTER 21

WHY DOES IT GET WEIRD WHEN YOU POINT OUT SOMETHING IS RACIST?

Have you tried pointing out that something is racist, or brought up racial justice with your teacher, parents, or friends? Maybe you brought it up at dinner one evening, and everyone scrunched up their noses like you did a smelly fart in the middle of the meal.

Some topics make people feel uncomfortable . . . but that's OK. It doesn't mean you have to stop talking about them. Fighting racism is important! You might need to find a different way to get into the conversation, though. It's like soccer. Sometimes you can just run down the wing, cut inside across the field, and score a goal! Other times, you have to pass, dodge, and tackle because your opponents have all their defenses up.

That's the thing about racism, especially with adults. People act like being *accused* of racism is as bad, or even worse, than *being* racist! They know it's bad to be racist, but they get caught up in thinking you are calling them a bad person. Or they might not know much about it and feel a bit embarrassed, so they shut the conversation down.

But remember: like in soccer, just because the other player has a good defense, it doesn't mean you give up. You have to keep pushing, keep playing, keep learning about and talking about how to fight racism. Eventually, you might score a goal or two. That will be something to celebrate!

Have you talked to your parent or caregiver about what you are reading and learning about in this book? If you haven't yet, maybe the next time they are in a good mood, you can share what you have discovered. Do they have stories of standing up and speaking out that they can share with you?

REMEMBER TO MAKE SURE YOU ARE SAFE!

If you have a friend or family member who you know has some very racist opinions, tackling it by yourself head-on might not always work. You can use something called the Socratic method—the "method of questions."

When someone—say, your uncle or grandmother—believes they are a good person, but they express a racist opinion, the trick is not to try to change their mind yourself but to get them to change their mind all on their own! How? Well, you ask lots of questions so that they can see the holes in their own thoughts. For example:

CHAPTER 22

I'M WHITE BUT MY LIFE HASN'T BEEN EASY! HOW COME PEOPLE CAN SAY THINGS TO ME AND IT'S NOT CONSIDERED RACIST?

If you are white, it can be hard to get your head around how life is for other people sometimes. It's also confusing: you might have a friend who is Black or South Asian, and their family has more money than you or lives in a nicer house . . . and then one day, they tell you that their life is more difficult because of racism and you have an "advantage" because you are white. You might think, *Huh? My life is hard! I don't get special treatment because I am white. What are you talking about?*

It's true. Your life may be hard. If it is, I am sorry. You might not have as much money, or get to fly to other countries, or even have enough food to eat every day, but someone who is another "race" does. The important point is this: your life is not hard because of your skin color but because of other factors. (These other reasons could be class, income, gender, sexuality, disability.)

We live in a world where, long ago, powerful people said that the white "race" was better than the others, so if you are white, you benefit from that. I call it "white priority." It gives you a head start (however you are traveling) in your journey up the mountain. Other things may hold you back, but your "race" won't be one of them.

If you woke up tomorrow and you were a different "race," do you think life would be harder or easier for you and your family?

But we want a world where everyone gets a fair chance, right? In order for that to happen, a lot of work still needs to be done. And you're part of making it happen!

CHAPTER 23

CAN YOU BE RACIST IF YOU ARE NOT WHITE?

Ah! We talked in chapter 5 about how prejudice or being mean to someone because they are white is hurtful but doesn't fit into our definition of "racism," because it doesn't have the POWER of history and society behind it. This doesn't mean it's OK! It just means that it is a different type of behavior (more like interpersonal bullying).

That being said, if you are putting someone down who is Black or any other "race" and you use the POWER of history and society, that is racism! You can experience racism from another brown person . . . the focus isn't on the person but on the act itself. So my Indian friend calling me names because I am Black is racist because whatever names are being used, whoever is using them, *those names* carry the weight and power of history to make me (and people like me) feel small.

SMASHED

STRUCK

BOMBED

A Cure for Racism?

Racism is a poison to which we can all be exposed, anywhere in the world. It's on the street, in school, and in stories. We can pass that poison on to others, through our words and actions, or we can take the antidote! Racial justice won't cure us right away, but if we take the medicine every day—in watching the way we think and behave— then we will slowly get rid of the racist toxins our brains have absorbed and help build a better, safer world for us all.

CHAPTER 24

I DON'T HAVE ANYBODY WHO IS DIFFERENT FROM ME IN MY SCHOOL OR TOWN. WHAT CAN I DO TO FIGHT RACISM?

When you live in a place where most people look like you, it can be hard to learn about other "races," cultures, and worlds. If there is a family in your school or town who is of a different "race," the first thing I would ask is: Are you and your family friends with them? Do you include them like you include everyone else? Or do you keep them at a bit of a distance because you think they are different and strange? If you are part of the dominant culture, it's your job to make sure they are welcome and feel safe—so you should start by doing that. It can be as simple as giving someone a big smile as you pass them in the street, or saying a cheery hello! If they are new in your area and the same age, maybe you can even ask them if they'd like to hang out!

Think about it—if you were the only one who was different in a school or town, wouldn't you want to know that you were welcome and safe?

Now that you have made sure that people feel safe in your community, you can start to learn about all the other communities in your area. Even if you really cannot find anyone from another community in your school or town, that doesn't have to stop you from learning more about other cultures and speaking out against racism.

Maybe do some research or ask your teacher (or the internet!) about the history of the area. Depending on where you are in the world, there may be Indigenous people who live in your area. Where are they? What is their relationship to the land? What are their customs? You can watch movies or TV shows from different parts of the world on YouTube, or videos on TikTok from different cultures (K-pop! Bollywood! Nollywood!), and you can even try to learn a new language to open you up to a new community. There is so much in the world to learn and explore . . . It's all about being generous, humble, and curious.

FIND OUT MORE
Have you ever heard of "Aotearoa"? It's the current Māori name for New Zealand. The Māori people are the Indigenous Polynesian people of mainland New Zealand. Why not look at countries all around the world and find out more about the Indigenous people living in those countries?

CHAPTER 25

WHAT ABOUT INSTITUTIONAL RACISM?

Remember the Circles of Power on page 89? The third circle from the center is the institutional stuff. Let's focus on an institution close to home, like school.

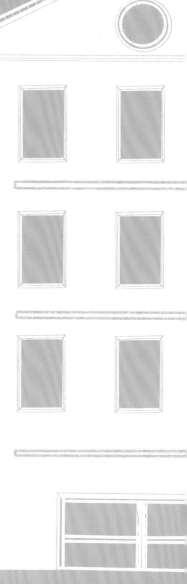

What do you learn at school? What books are you reading? Do they only have white characters? Or are the stories that they tell about Black and brown people always super sad? We can be happy too! What do you learn about the history of the United States or about the amazing civilizations that existed outside Europe? Does your school celebrate Black History Month? Could you push for it to be extended throughout the school year? (Black people exist all year round!)

Why not ask if the school can book guest speakers? Or suggest that you study the Indigenous history of your local area, or research anti-racism leaders around the world and learn how they went about making change.

1. Name the rule that needs changing, and figure out exactly what the new rule should be. (No halal/kosher food? The new rule should be to make halal and kosher food available at school!)

2. Get people on your side: start with your friends, if you want, and then your class, and then go bigger! Ask your teacher if you can speak about it in homeroom, and maybe set up a petition.

3. Present your idea to a supportive adult who can take it to the school leaders—maybe it is your teacher, maybe someone else at school who can help. Don't be afraid to ask!

Perhaps you can do a presentation in class about one of these leaders.

Look at the rules! In a school, you have lots of power to change the rules that affect students. Does your school have a racial justice policy? Does your school have a dress code that is fair for people with **_4c hair_**? Does your swim team encourage kids who wear the hijab? Think about the rules that are around you and ask for them to be made fair for everyone, not just white people from the dominant culture.

CHAPTER 26

WHY IS RACISM SO HARD TO STOP?

Racism has been going on for a long, long time. Part of the reason it's hard to get rid of is that some people benefit from it, and they don't want to give up their advantage. The reality is, even if folks don't know it yet, getting rid of racism is ultimately good for everyone. It makes for a healthier, safer, more prosperous society for us all.

Here's what I want you to remember: racism was created by humans, and it can be—and will be—destroyed by humans as well. And there has been so much progress over the centuries. So much has actually changed! We stand on the shoulders of giants, folks who have fought (and sometimes died) for the rights and freedoms we enjoy today. So, really, we're just doing our part, you feel me? They passed the racial justice baton on to us. It's our turn to run with it!

Change, Change, Change

Changes in society don't always happen in days, or months, or even years. They can sometimes happen over decades, and even centuries. We might not always get to see the changes we are making. But remember: you don't have to change the whole world. You only have to focus on changing the world around you. The world of your friends, family, teachers, teammates—if each and every one of us focuses on changing our world, then together, with our powers combined, well, that's pretty world-changing, isn't it?

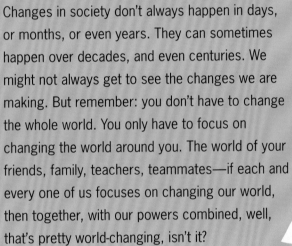
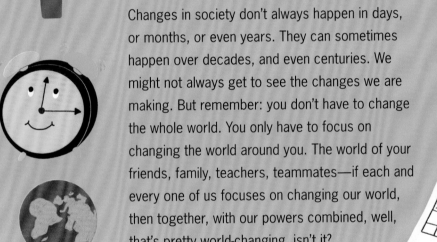

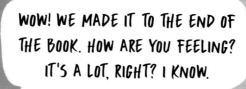

WOW! WE MADE IT TO THE END OF THE BOOK. HOW ARE YOU FEELING? IT'S A LOT, RIGHT? I KNOW.

It can feel overwhelming sometimes, taking everything in: about why racism started, the impact it is having, and what we need to do to fix it. I get overwhelmed myself sometimes. It's OK! It is important to acknowledge that we have a big challenge ahead of us. However, I want you to have hope. Each and every one of us has a part to play in making this world a fairer, safer world for us all.

NICE VIEW, HUH?

At the start of the book we thought about life as being like an imaginary mountain that was harder for some people to climb than for others . . .

Maybe you can think of this book like it's a map that shows you all the different routes that people can take to make that climb fairer for everyone. Now that you have the map, it's up to you how you share that knowledge with other people, and how to find your way along the best route for you.

It's been wonderful going on this journey with you. See you out there, and good luck, inshallah!

HOW TO GET INSPIRED

Reading this book might be the first time you've seen the term "racial justice," but people have been standing up and speaking out against racism for a very long time—and today there are many, many other people writing and talking about racial justice.

WHO?

For example, you could look up Stuart Hall, who was one of the most influential writers on how "race" affects how you interact with the world. If you want to learn more about the history and power behind Black women's hair, you could look up Emma Dabiri's *Don't Touch My Hair*. Then there's Mariam Khan, a Muslim journalist who speaks out against Islamophobia and has edited a collection of essays called *It's Not About the Burqa*. Maybe you're interested in watching movies made by Black creators, like American director Ava DuVernay and British filmmaker Steve McQueen, that center Black characters telling their own stories.

WHEN?

WHERE?

HOW?

One of the easiest ways to continue on the journey toward racial justice is to be curious! Find out more about other people's experiences and learn to see the world through their eyes.

If you like sports, why not find out more about prominent sports personalities from different backgrounds and consider the additional challenges they faced to get where they are? You could do the same for actors, musicians, or authors.

TALK TO THE PEOPLE YOU LIVE WITH

Maybe you're super into science and engineering (like I am!) but haven't considered which scientists or engineers get the most attention. Did you know many modern medical innovations started in the Muslim world? People in Istanbul received early forms of vaccinations years before they became the norm in England. Whether it's vaccinations, prescription glasses, or even knowledge about how the heart works, modern medicine would look very different if it weren't for Muslim scientists. Wild, huh?

Why not expand that search and investigate activists who are fighting for racial justice all around the world today? As you've learned in this book, racism shows up in many different shapes and sizes, and the things that you need to stand up to where you live might be totally different from the issues that someone else is speaking out against in India, Brazil, or my own country, Sudan. But no matter where we are in the world, we can learn from each other and be united in solidarity against all forms of social injustice in the world.

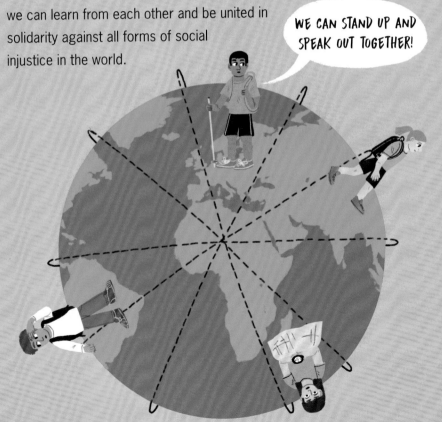

WE CAN STAND UP AND SPEAK OUT TOGETHER!

GLOSSARY

4c hair: hair with a thick texture that forms the tightest, densest curls

abolish: to put an end to something. When we talk about abolishing slavery, we mean the process by which the institution of slavery was taken apart and people were stopped from owning slaves. Eventually, this led to those enslaved people being freed.

antisemitism: prejudice toward and discrimination against someone for being Jewish

autonomous: having full control over what you do

bias: an instinct (sometimes conscious, sometimes not) that steers you toward preferring one thing over another

chattel slavery: chattel refers to something a person owns. In this instance, it means that someone "owned" the Black people, who were stripped of any choice or freedom and taken to work as slaves.

citizen: someone who "belongs" to a particular country. Being a citizen of a country can mean that you are legally allowed to do things like work, pay taxes and vote.

colonizing: going to a different country, taking control over that country, and calling it your own

colorism: prejudice toward and discrimination against someone because of the shade of their skin. It is a term usually applied within a "racial" group, when people with lighter skin receive better treatment than those with darker skin.

community: a group made up of people who all have something in common. It can be applied to different sizes of groups. Someone could refer to the Black community, covering all Black people, or the school community, meaning all the people who go to that school.

compensation: something that is awarded to make up for a loss of some kind

deport: to force someone out of the country in which they are living

diaspora: a community of people whose families come from the same country but now live all around the world

discrimination: the treatment of someone differently (usually for the worse)

dominant culture: a particular set of attitudes and background that's given priority and considered "normal" within a country

enslaving: denying a person their freedom, treating them as less than human, and forcing them to work for free, without reward or recognition, usually under horrible conditions

equality: the state of everything being shared in exactly the same way, regardless of what is needed

equity: a way to achieve equality by making sure each person receives the correct treatment or tools they need to participate

ethnicity: the group you identify as part of, typically because of your family ancestry, culture, language, traditions, and more

eugenics: the scientifically disproven theory that humans can be "improved" by selecting who should live and die and have children (based on a made-up set of "ideals")

First Nations: a term used most often in Canada and Australia referring to the "original custodians" or "original people" of the land, the first known inhabitants. Sometimes also known as *Indigenous* people.

genocide: the deliberate killing or serious harming of a particular group of people because of their "race," religion, ethnicity, or nationality, with the intent to destroy the group

Holocaust: the mass killing (genocide) of Jewish people during the Second World War. Also known as the *Shoah*.

immigrant: someone who moves to another country and makes it their home

imperialist: a more powerful country or society that forcibly takes political and/or economic control over another country or society

Indigenous: see *First Nations*

inequality: the state of things not being shared evenly

institution: a large organization or social structure that deals with many different people

internalized: when thoughts and emotions are kept inside of us, allowing us to tell ourselves stories

interpersonal: between two or more people

intersect: to cross over, overlap, or meet. For instance, if you are Black and disabled, you are affected by racism (because you are Black) and ableism (because you are disabled): you are the point where both issues intersect.

Islamophobia: prejudice toward and discrimination against someone for being Muslim

justice: the completely fair treatment of everyone

legacy: something in the past that continues to affect the present

liberated: set free

marginalized: existing outside of the mainstream. In this book we talk about marginalized communities, meaning those that are not considered part of the dominant culture and have been historically oppressed and deliberately pushed to the margins.

meritocracy: a system that rewards people based on the effort that they put in, not on who they are or where they come from. This can sometimes be a trick word, because it hides the fact that not everyone starts from the same spot, gets treated the same way, or has the same resources. So while a meritocracy might be good in a fair and just world, we are not quite there yet.

microaggression: a way of exhibiting discrimination toward a group of people that's considered "subtle" by the dominant culture. For example, commenting on someone's choice of food as being "weird" when that food is something from outside the dominant culture and/or of a historically marginalized community.

migrating: leaving one country to settle in another

nationality: the status of belonging to the nation, or country, in which you have citizenship

Native nations: see *First Nations*

oppress: to treat a person or a particular group of people in an unjust, often cruel way, denying them equal freedoms and rights

policy: a specific set of ideas or a plan used as a guide for making decisions, particularly those within an institution

prejudice: a judgment a person makes about something or someone without having interacted with them

racialized: when the mechanism of "race" is applied to a particular group of people, even though they may not usually be considered one single "race." For example, all Muslims do not belong to one "race," but they are often treated as if they do by racist systems.

reparations: money paid by a country's government to make up for the harm it has caused other countries or groups of people

selective reporting: sharing only the facts that one wants other people to know

Shoah: the Hebrew word for the term "Holocaust," referring to the mass killing (genocide) of Jewish people during the Second World War

slur: an insult that hurts and shames someone

stereotype: a specific but widely held belief that groups people together, even though that belief might not be true of anyone in that group

systemic: part of a network made up of interconnected parts. A systemic issue is an issue that affects all of those parts.

treaty: a written agreement between two or more countries about what to do

white supremacist hierarchy: a system that places white people at the top and other "races" below

INDEX

A

abolishing slavery 29, 31, 122
Africa
  and European colonization 20–21
  Scramble for 20–21
Aliens Act 27
anti-racism policy/strategy 97, 114
antisemitism 44–45, 122

B

Barbados Slave Code 18
Berlin Conference 20
Black history 114
  in Britain 26
  in the US 26
British Empire 27, 29, 97

C

chattel slavery 26, 122
Chinese Exclusion Act 26
Circles of Power 89, 114
citizenship 35, 124
civil rights movement 29
colonialism/colonization 14–15, 17, 18, 22, 24, 25, 26–27, 30, 48, 49, 63, 82, 122
  British 26–27, 32
  European 14–15, 24, 30, 48, 49
  roots of racism 14–22, 24–27, 40–41, 48
colorism 25, 122
compensation 31, 32, 33, 122
  see also reparations

D

deportation 27, 122
diaspora 37, 122
dominant culture 24–25, 38–39, 40, 42, 53, 54, 66–67, 112–113, 123
  and institutions 58, 66, 68
  see also systemic advantage

E

education 25, 56, 65–67, 114–115
Empire Windrush 27
empires. See British Empire; colonialism/colonization; imperialism
equality 76, 123
equity 77, 123
ethnicity 8, 20, 34–37, 66, 68, 86, 90, 112–113, 123
eugenics 45, 123

F

First Nations people 26, 36, 123
  see also Indigenous people

G

genocide 44–45, 123, 125

H

hijab 8, 57, 75, 115
Holocaust 33, 44–45, 123, 125

I

imperialism 17, 20–21, 29, 48–49, 123
Indigenous people 26, 82, 113, 114, 123
  see also First Nations people
institutional racism 50–51, 56–57, 58–59, 60, 64–67, 89, 114–115
  see also education; law enforcement; media
internalized racism 50–53, 60, 64, 66, 69, 73, 89, 90–91
interpersonal racism 50–51, 54–55, 64, 66, 89, 92–95
Islamophobia 43, 74, 75, 120, 124

L

law enforcement 65, 68–69

M

media (news, social media, TV, movies, and books) 25, 38, 51, 52, 65, 68, 69, 70, 71, 73, 86, 87, 91, 97, 113, 120

meritocracy 77, 124
migration/migrating 26,
    124

N
nationality 34–37, 124

P
police. *See* law
    enforcement

R
race
    and categories 18, 36
    and colonialism 15, 18,
        24, 27, 28, 48
    and ethnicity and
        nationality 34–37
    and Muslims 42–43
    racialization 23, 42, 44,
        45, 125
    as a social invention
        15, 18, 22, 23, 29,
        34, 48
    and standards of beauty
        52–53, 57
    and stereotypes 72–73,
        86–87
racism
    and bias/prejudice
        38–41, 53
    deep roots of 16–17,
        28–29, 30–31, 63,
        73, 116–117
    and hair 15, 51, 52,
        56–57, 70, 99, 115,
        120, 122

and institutions 25, 45,
    56, 59, 68
and law 15, 18, 48
modern manifestations
    of 50–69
origins of 14–23, 24
standing up against
    80–81, 88–99,
    116–117
throughout the world
    24–27, 44–45, 57,
    75
see also
    institutional racism;
    internalized racism;
    interpersonal racism;
    systemic racism
religion 42–44, 74–75,
    115
reparations 31, 32, 33,
    49, 125
representation 70–71, 87
    and the Houses of
        Parliament 58–59
    and the US Congress 59

S
selective reporting 68, 69,
    72, 125
Shoah, the 44–45, 123,
    125
Slave Compensation Act
    32
    see also compensation;
        reparations
slavery 14, 16, 17, 18,
    20, 22
    abolishing 29, 122
    and Brazil 27

and the National Trust
    (UK) 32
origins 14
and the US 26, 28, 68
see also chattel slavery
sports 71, 72–73, 75, 89,
    120
stereotypes 45, 66, 67,
    71, 72–73, 74,
    86–87, 125
systemic advantage
    39–41, 60–63, 108
systemic racism 50–51,
    60–63, 64, 87, 89

T
third culture 37

U
US history 97, 114

W
White Australia policy 26
white supremacy 25, 29,
    31, 48–49, 50, 53,
    64, 73, 125